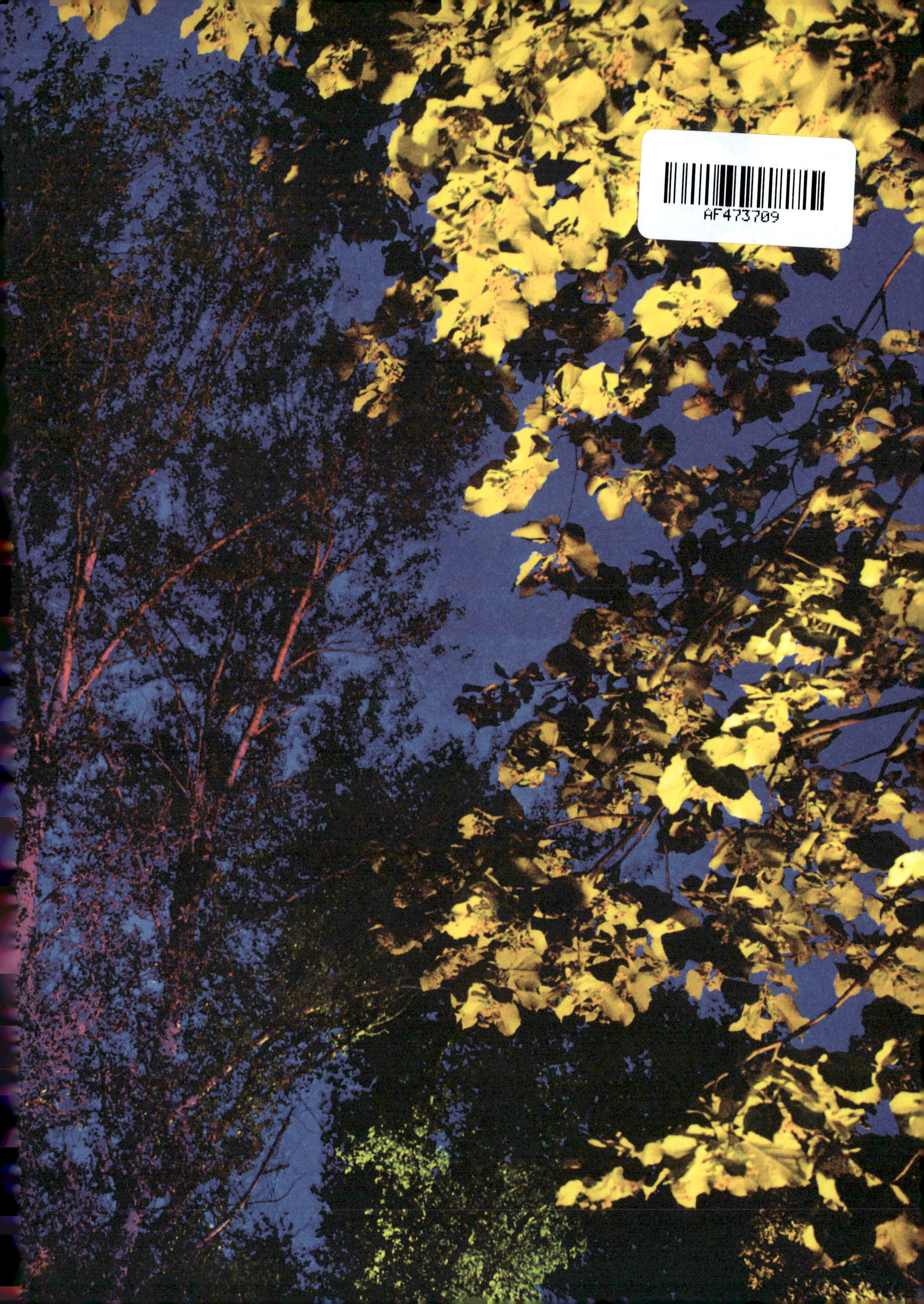

Archipiélago

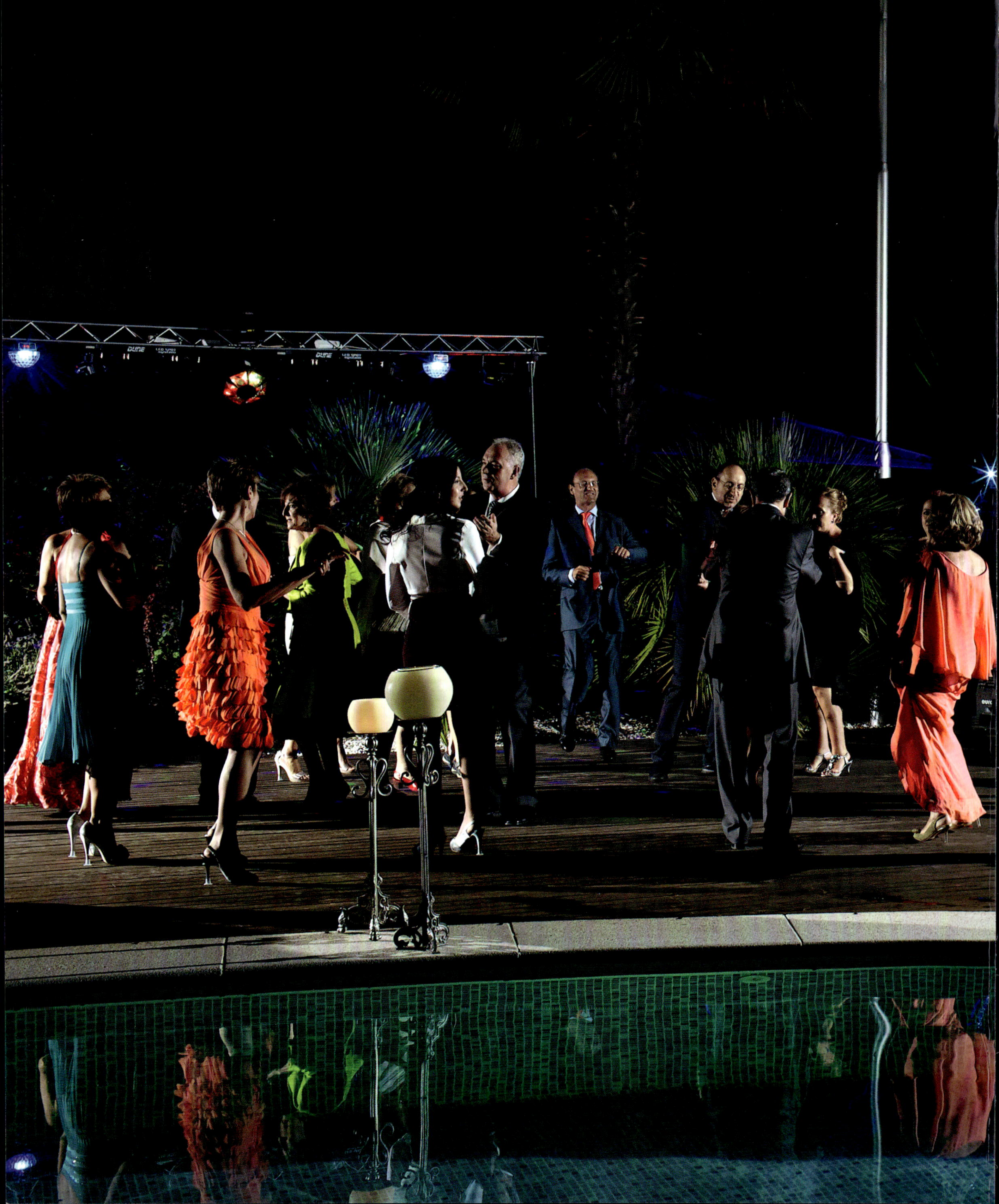
DUNE
LED SPOT
DUNE
LED SPOT

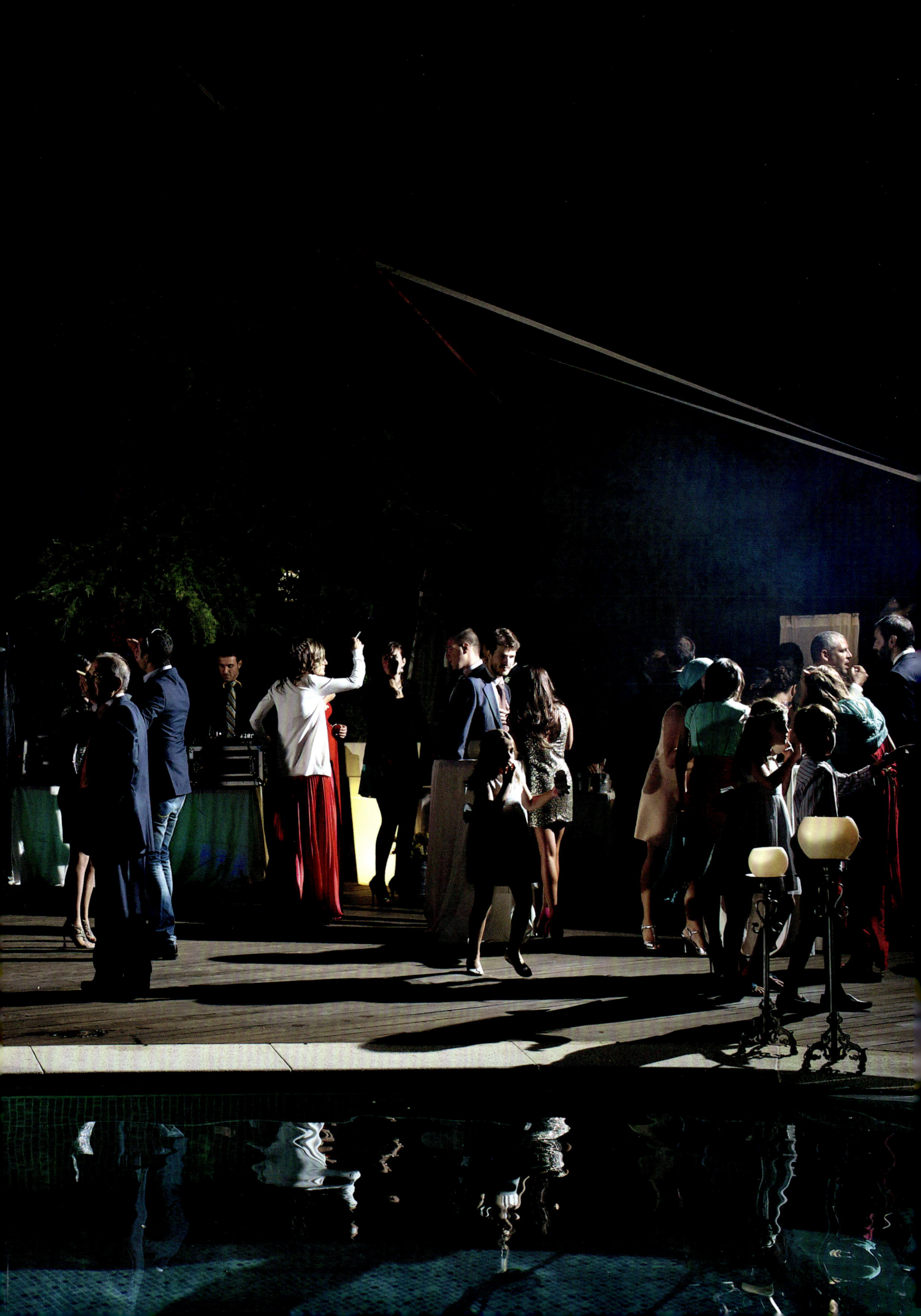

Hugo Alcol

Verlag Kettler

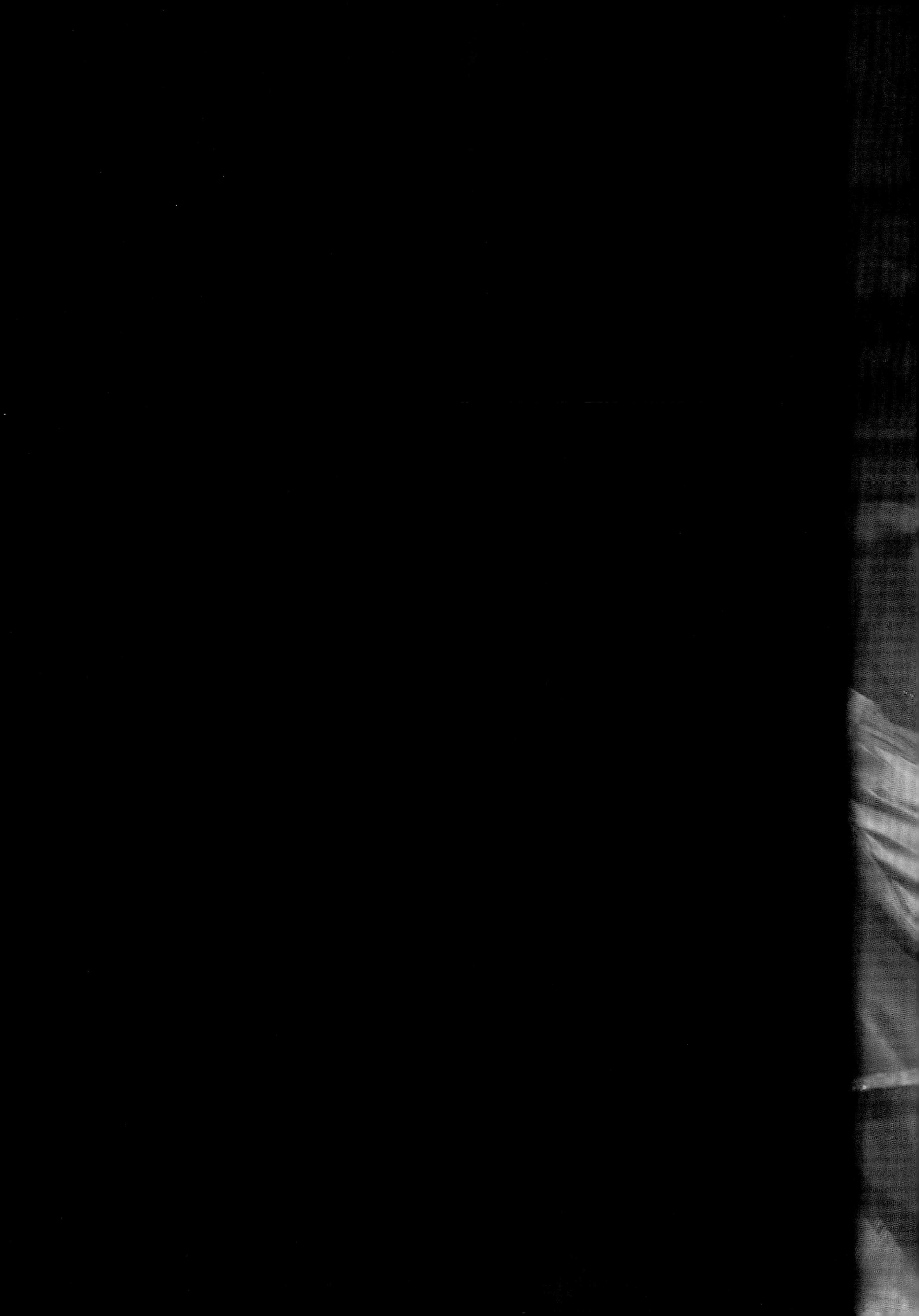

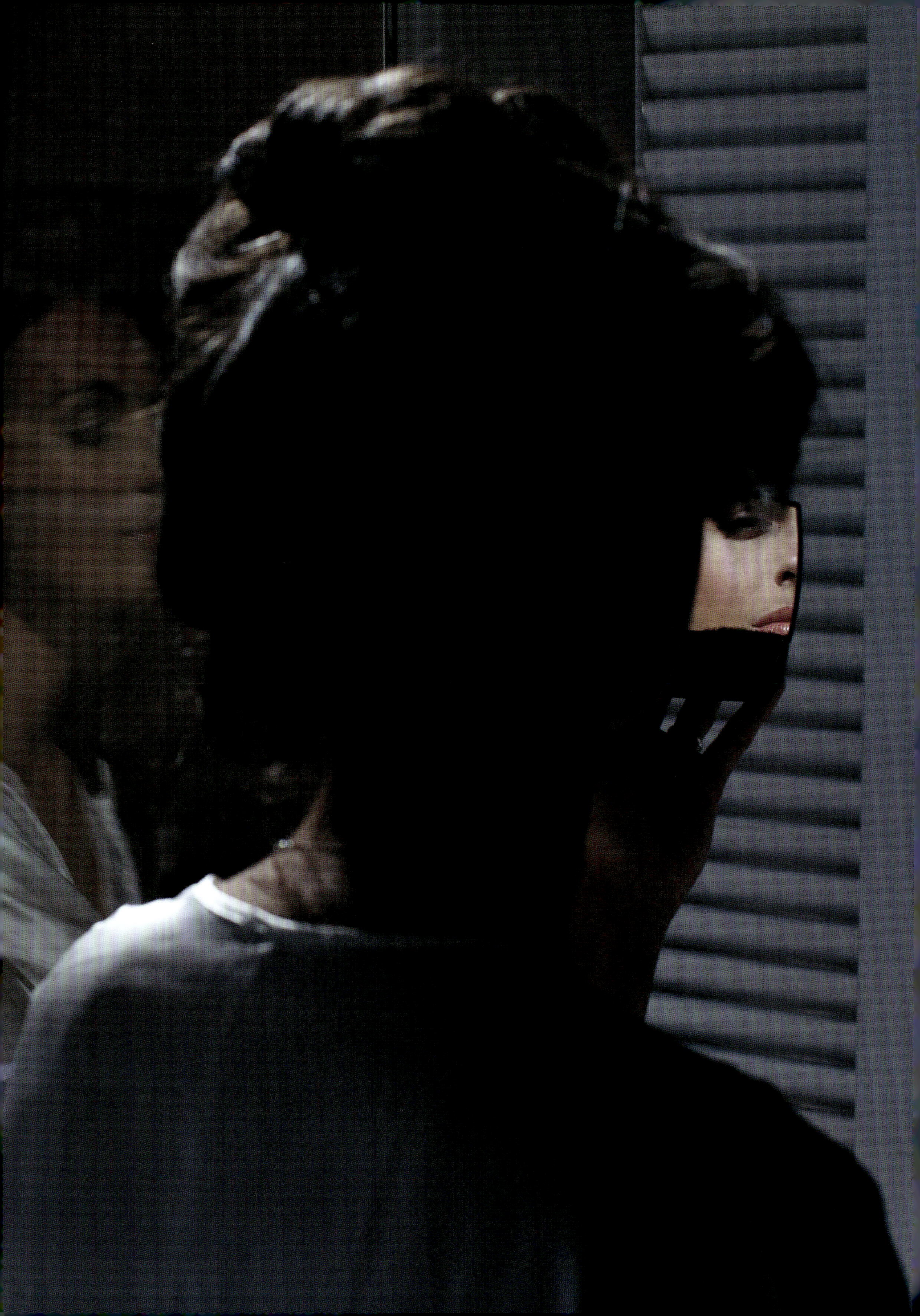

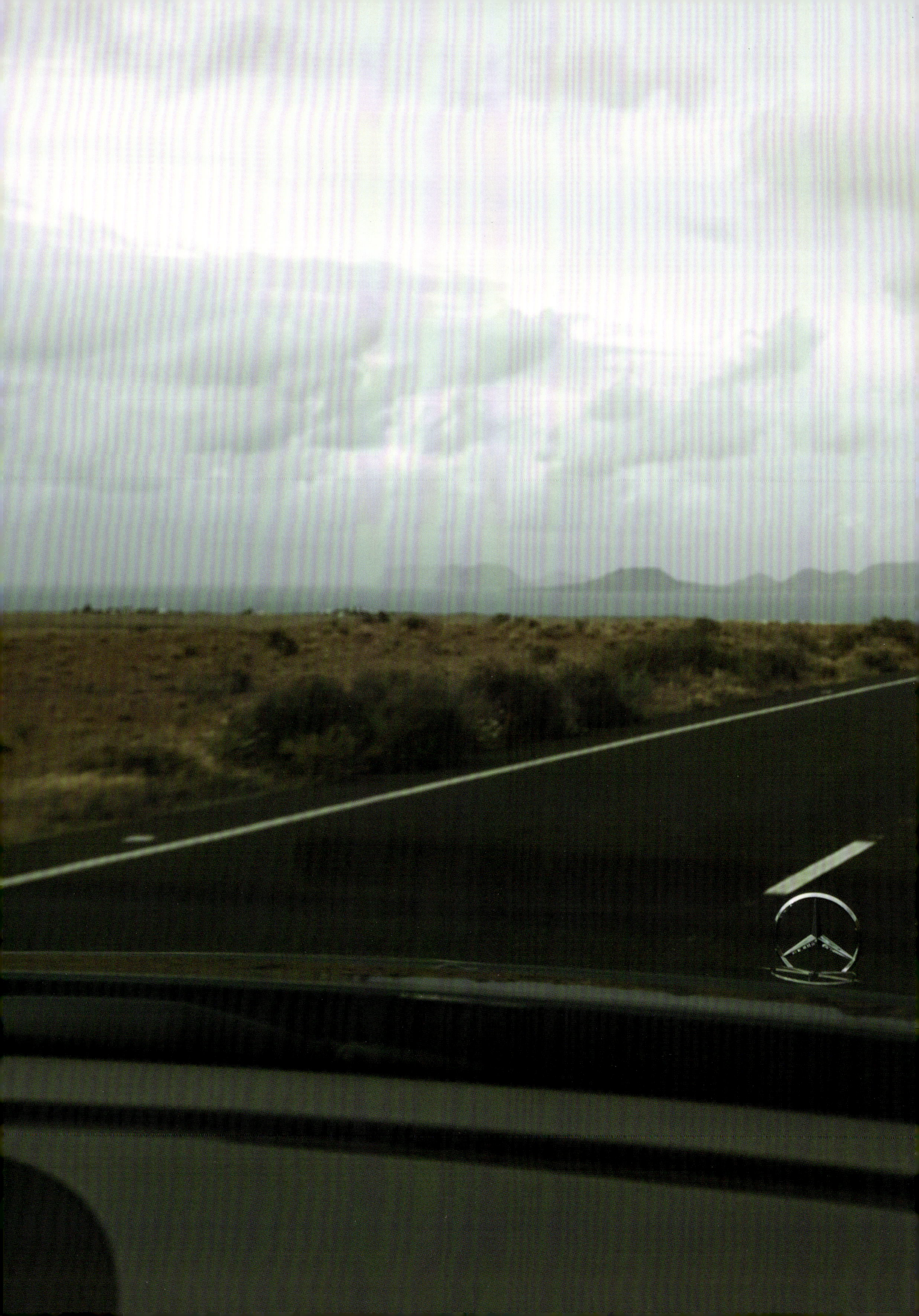

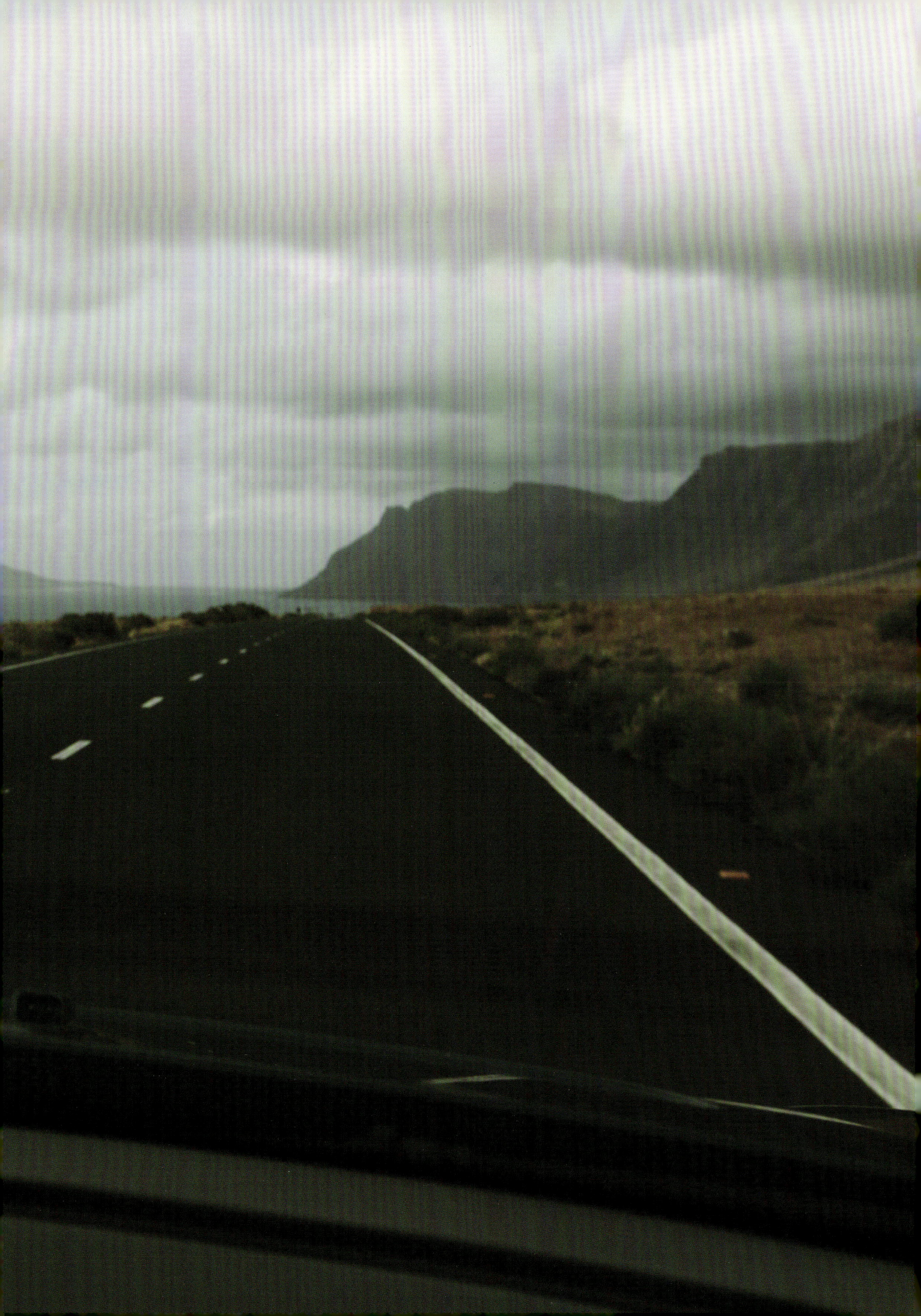

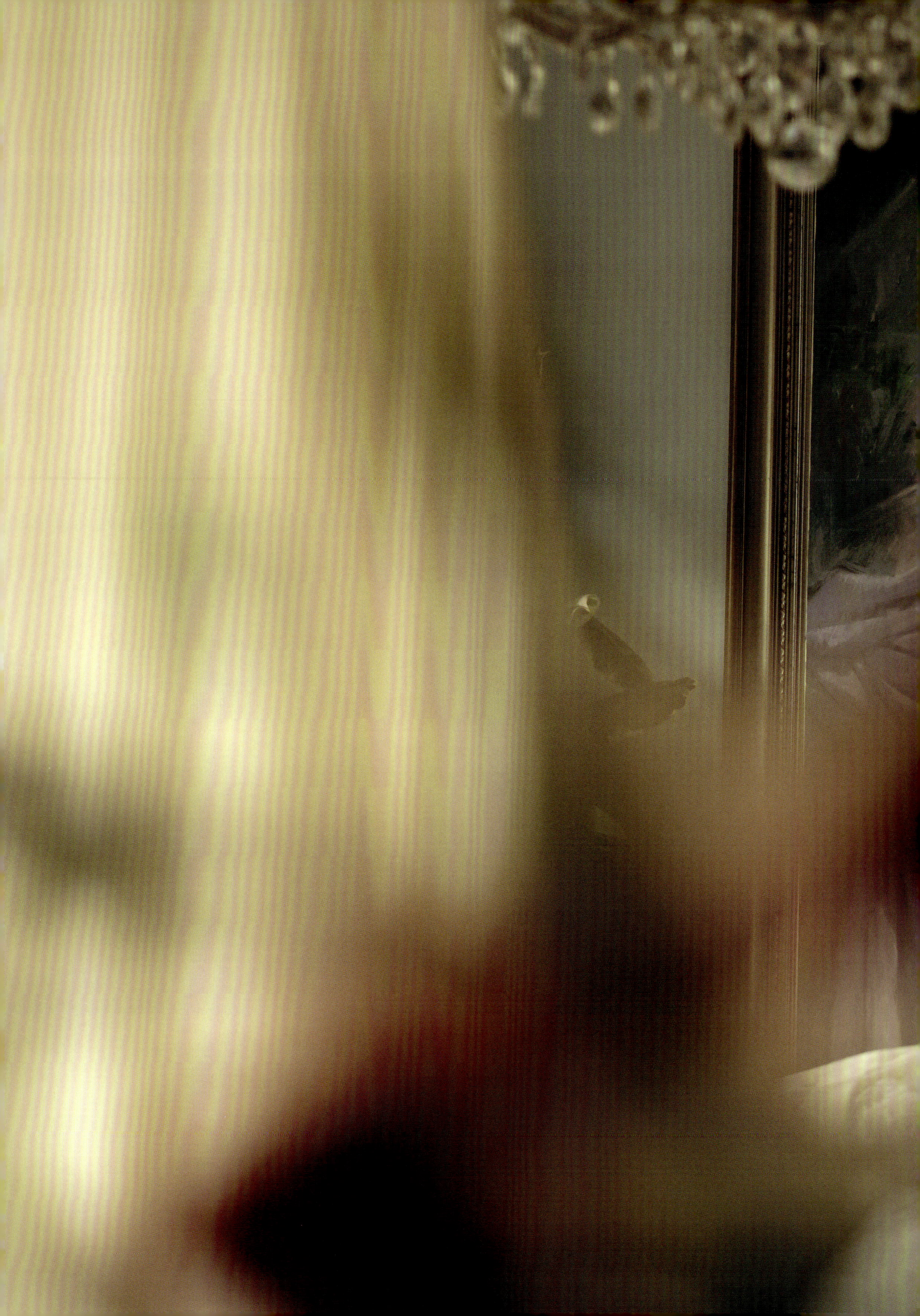

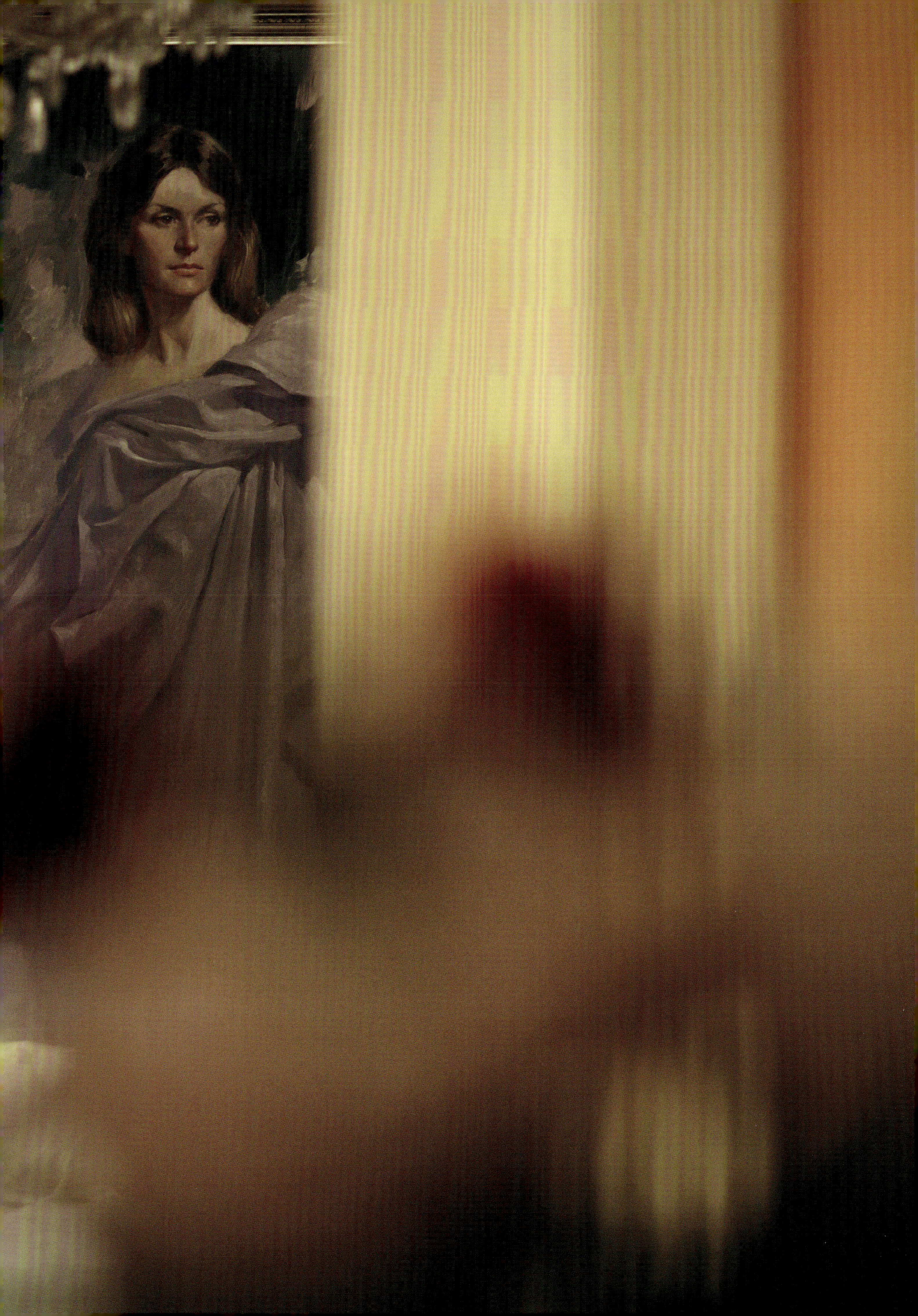

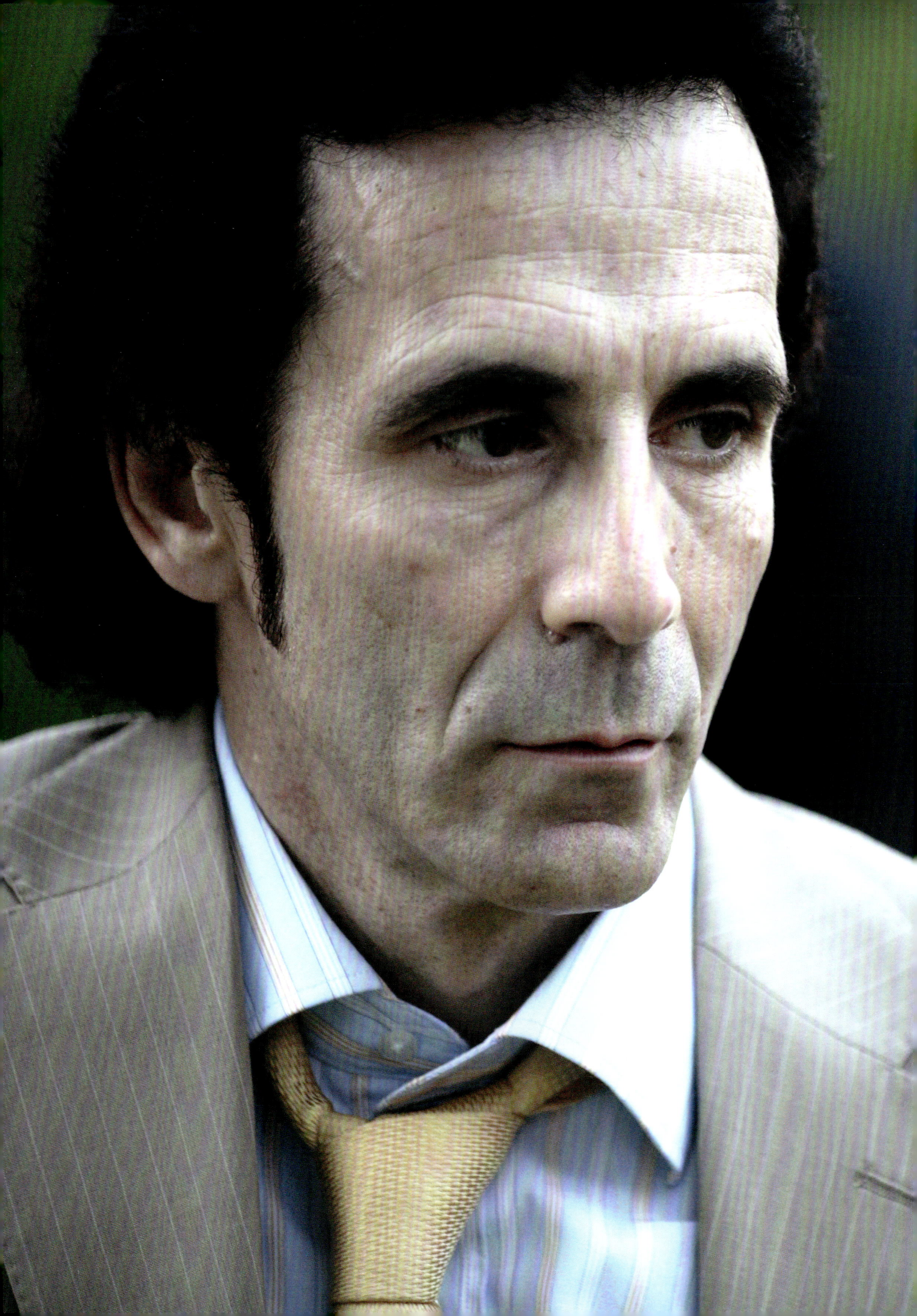

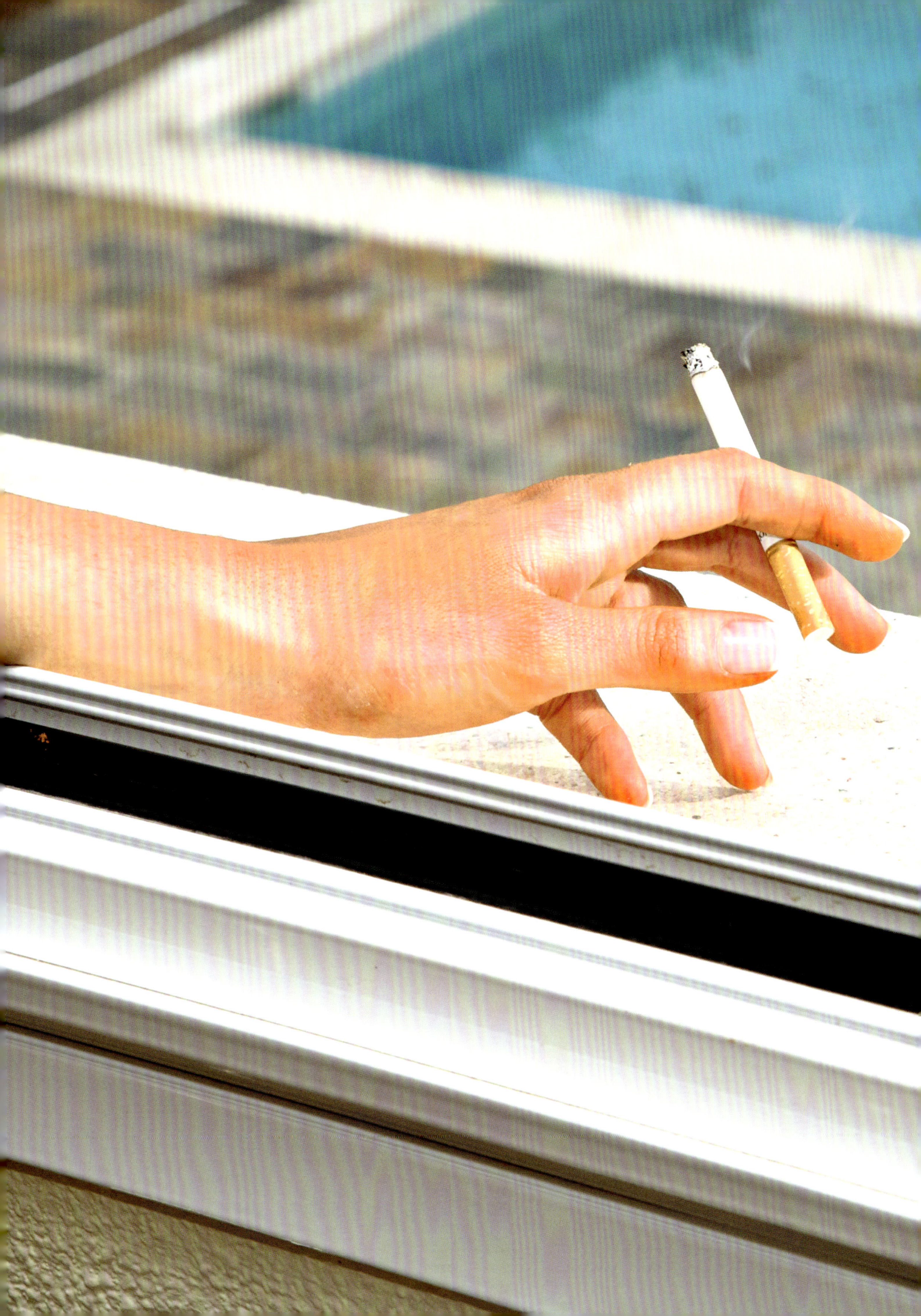

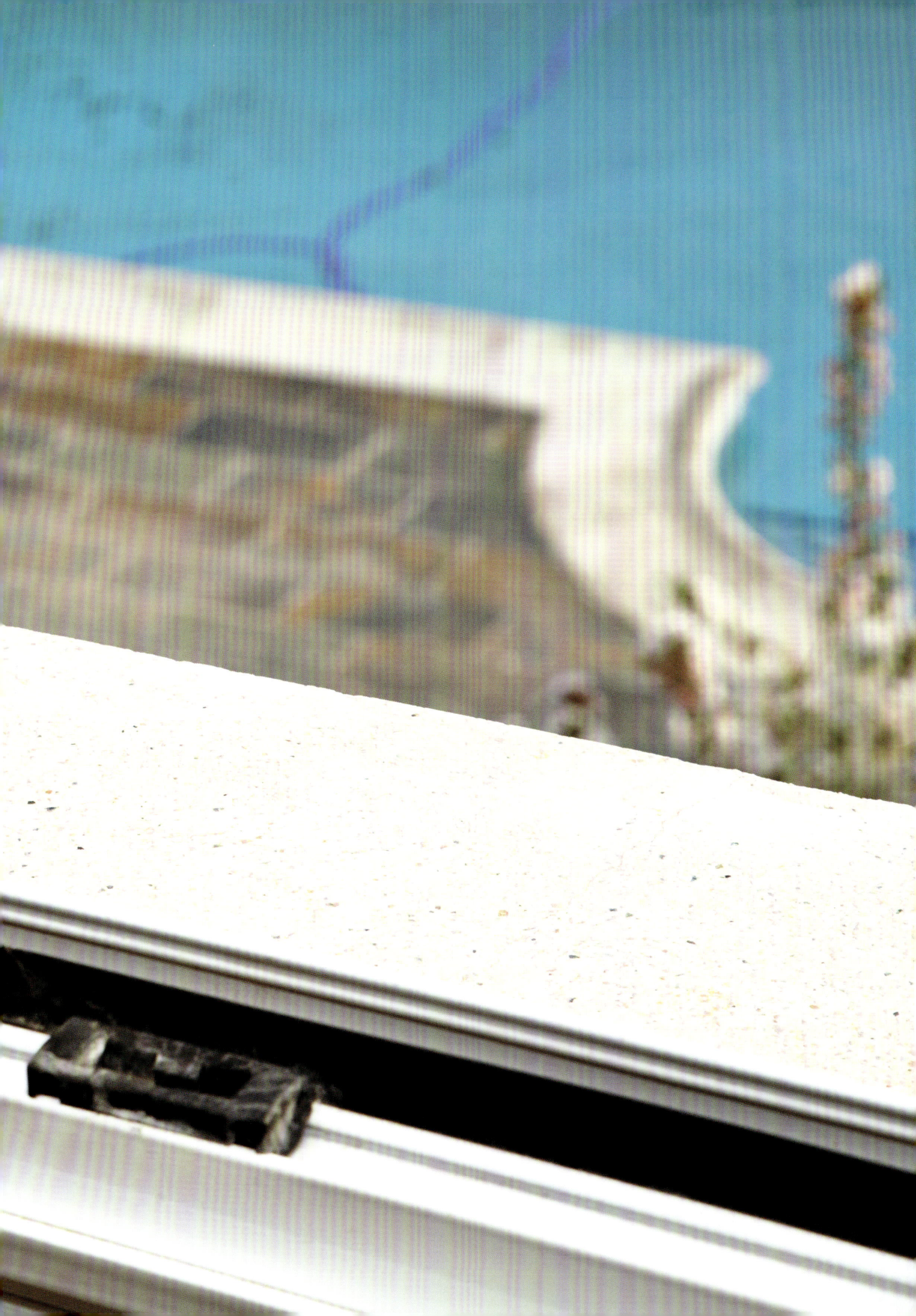

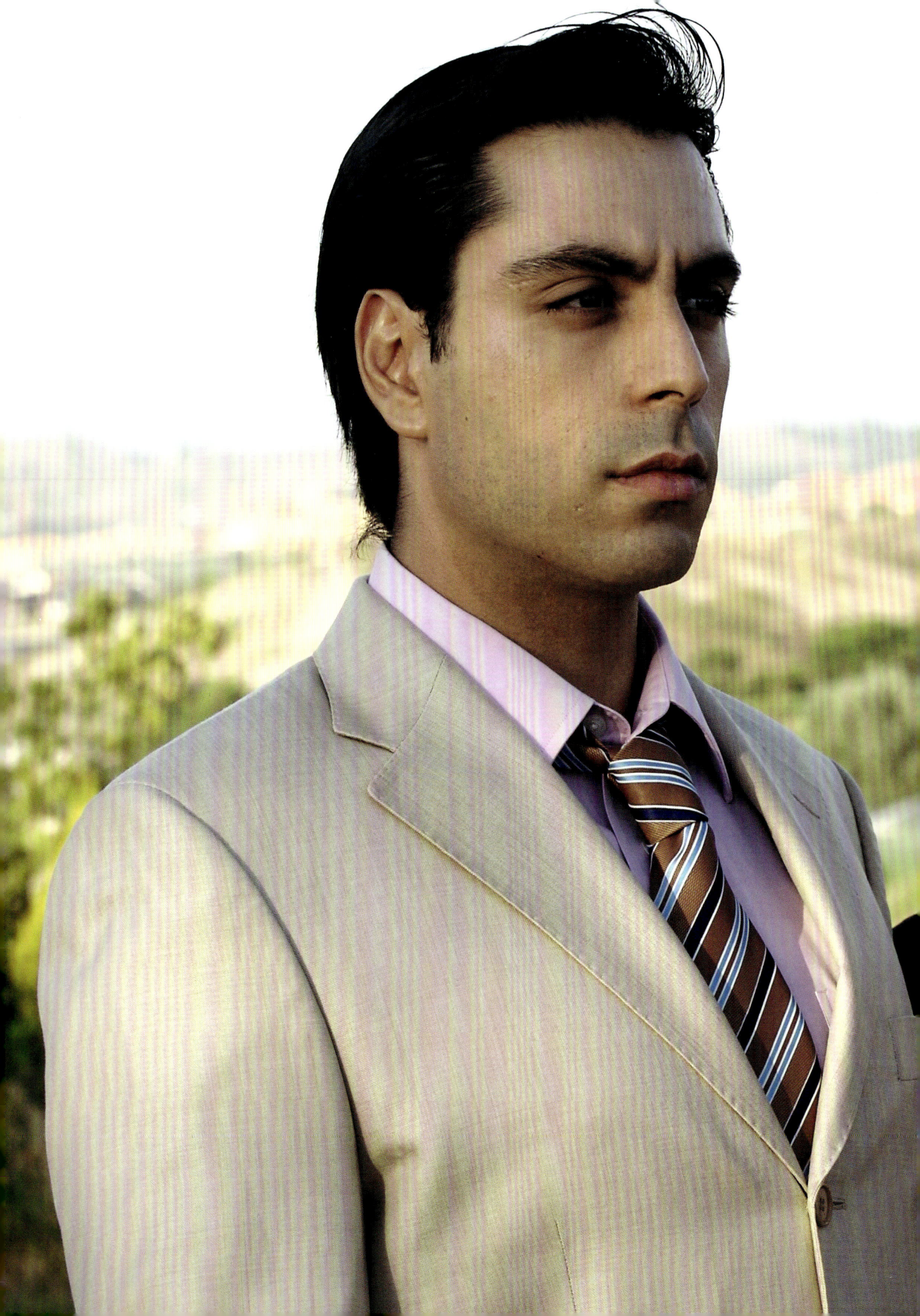

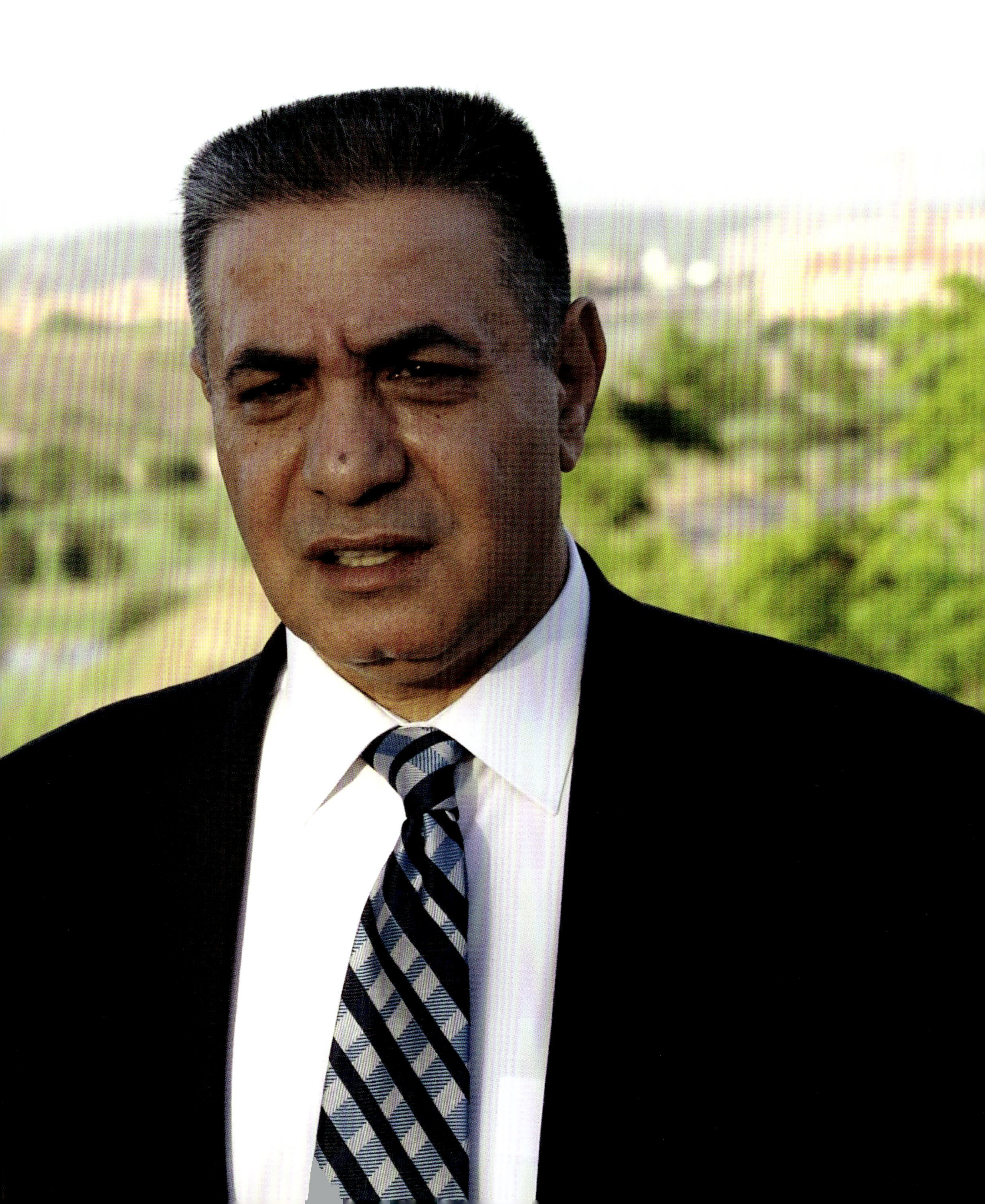

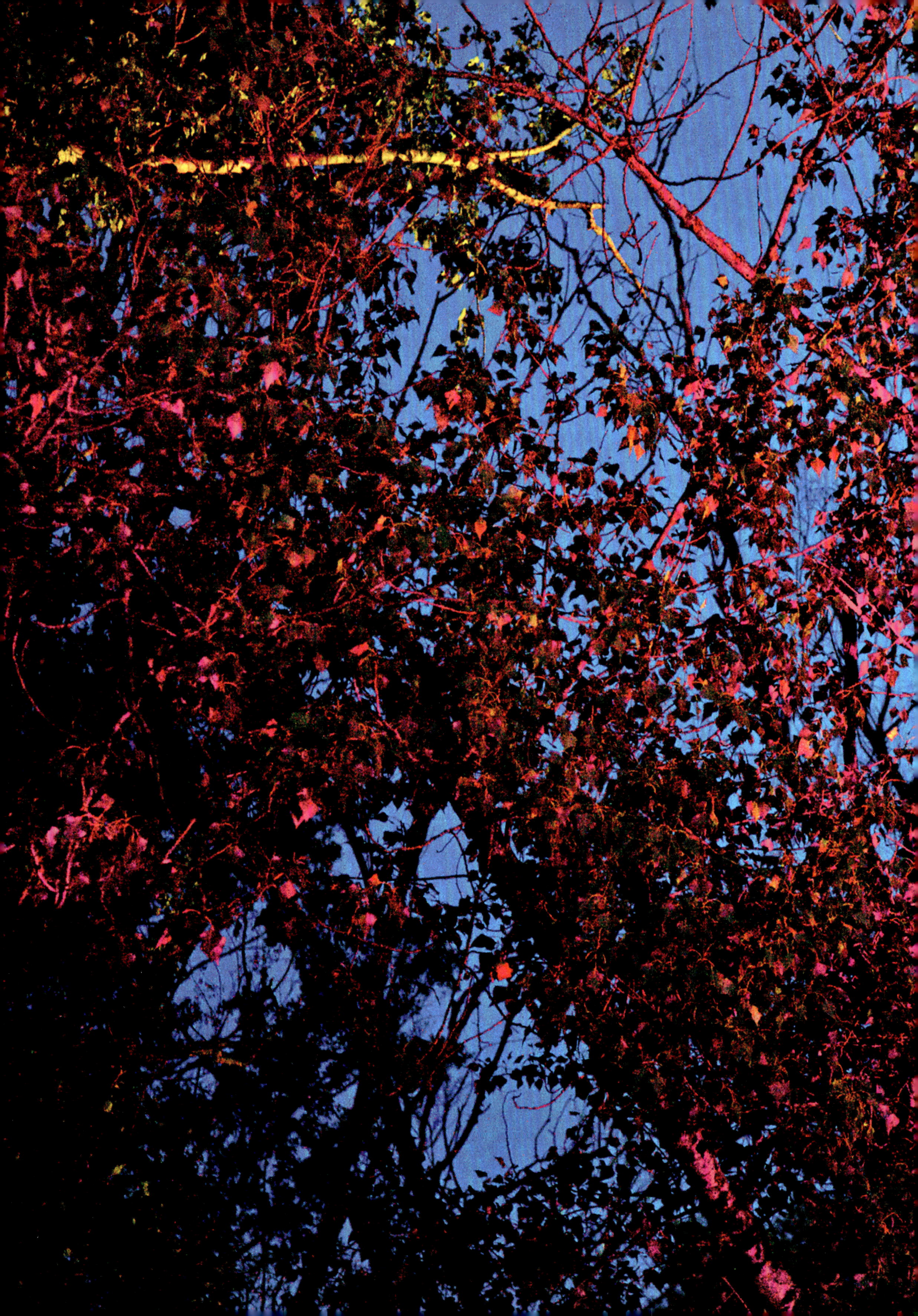

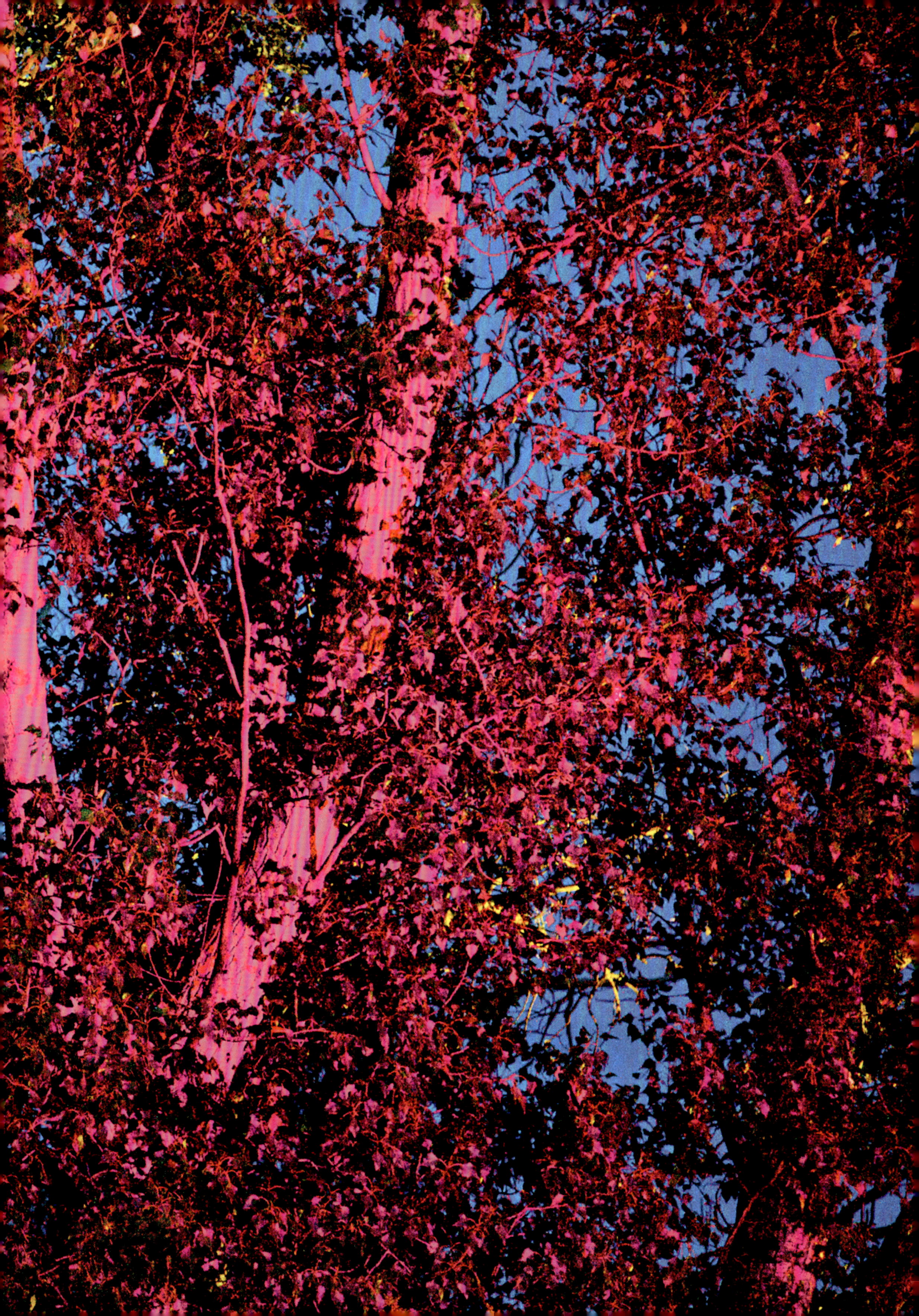

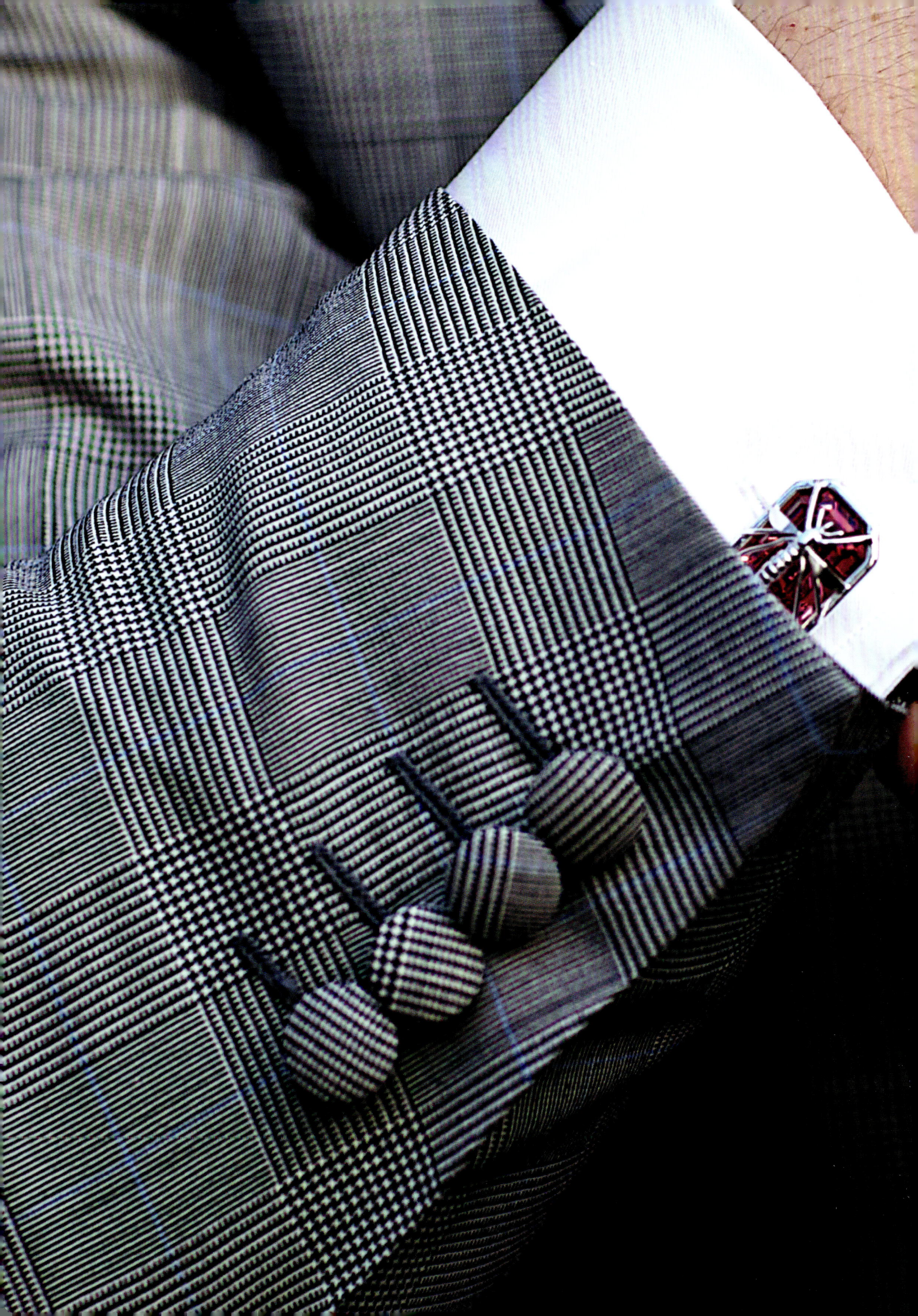

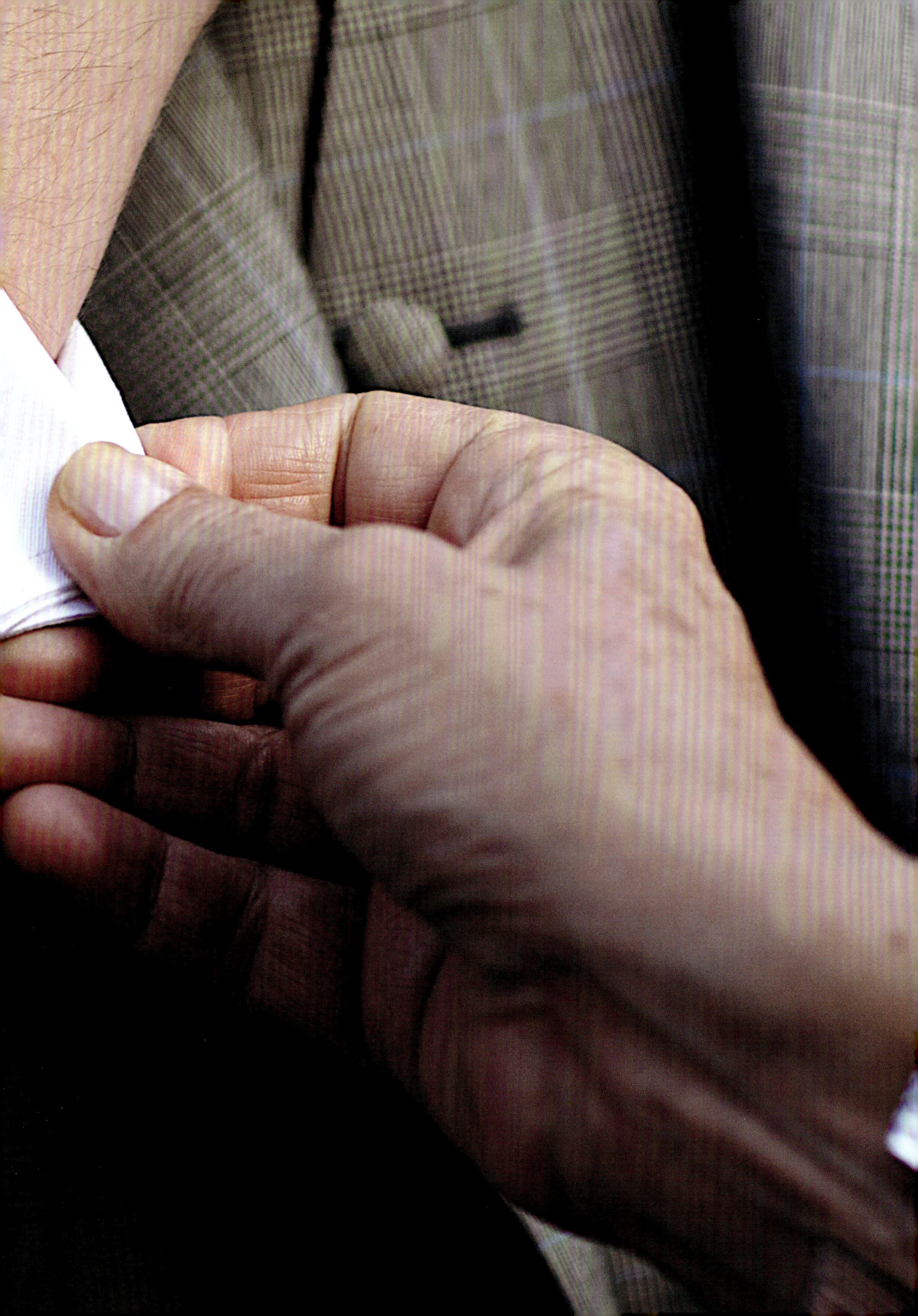

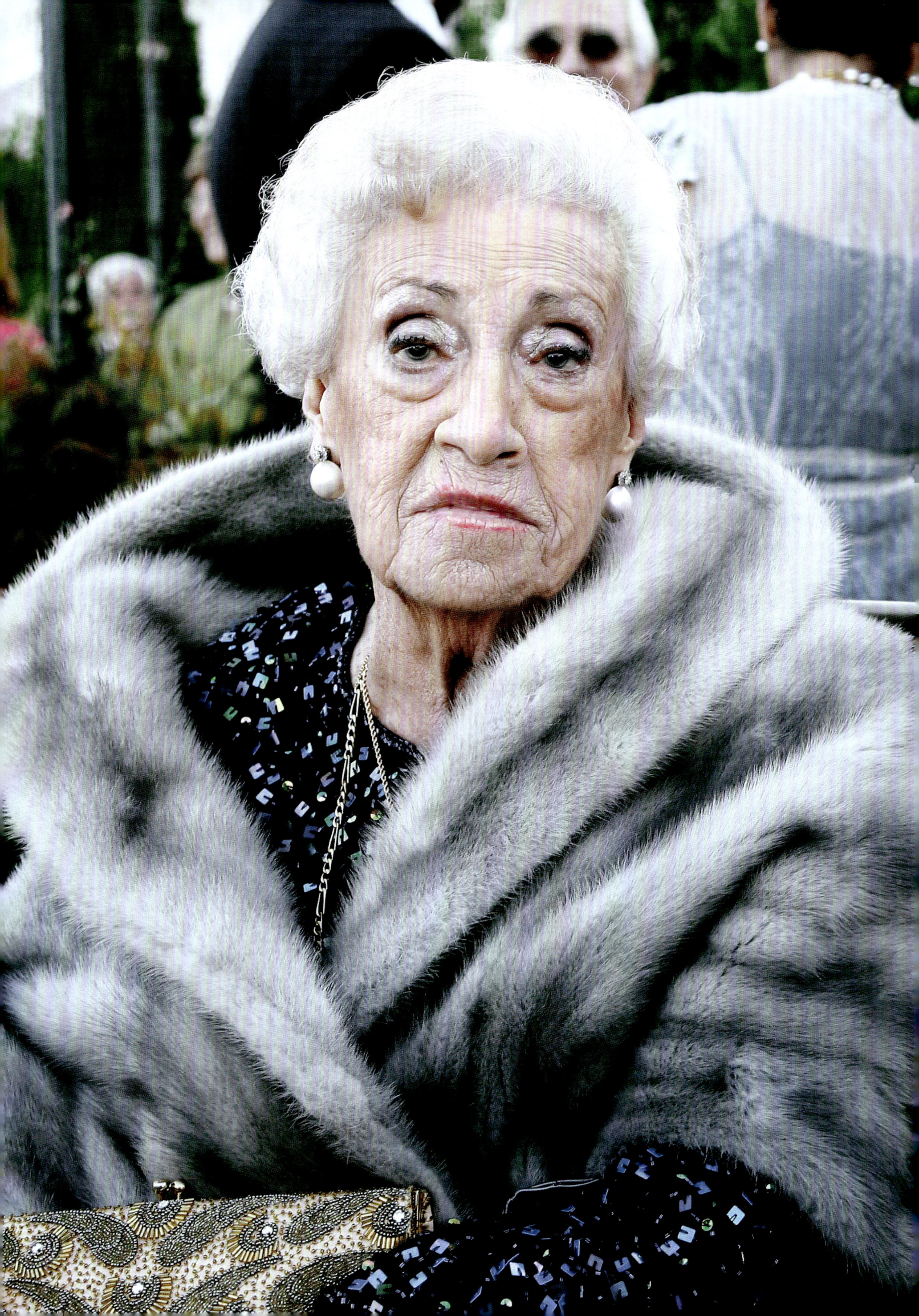

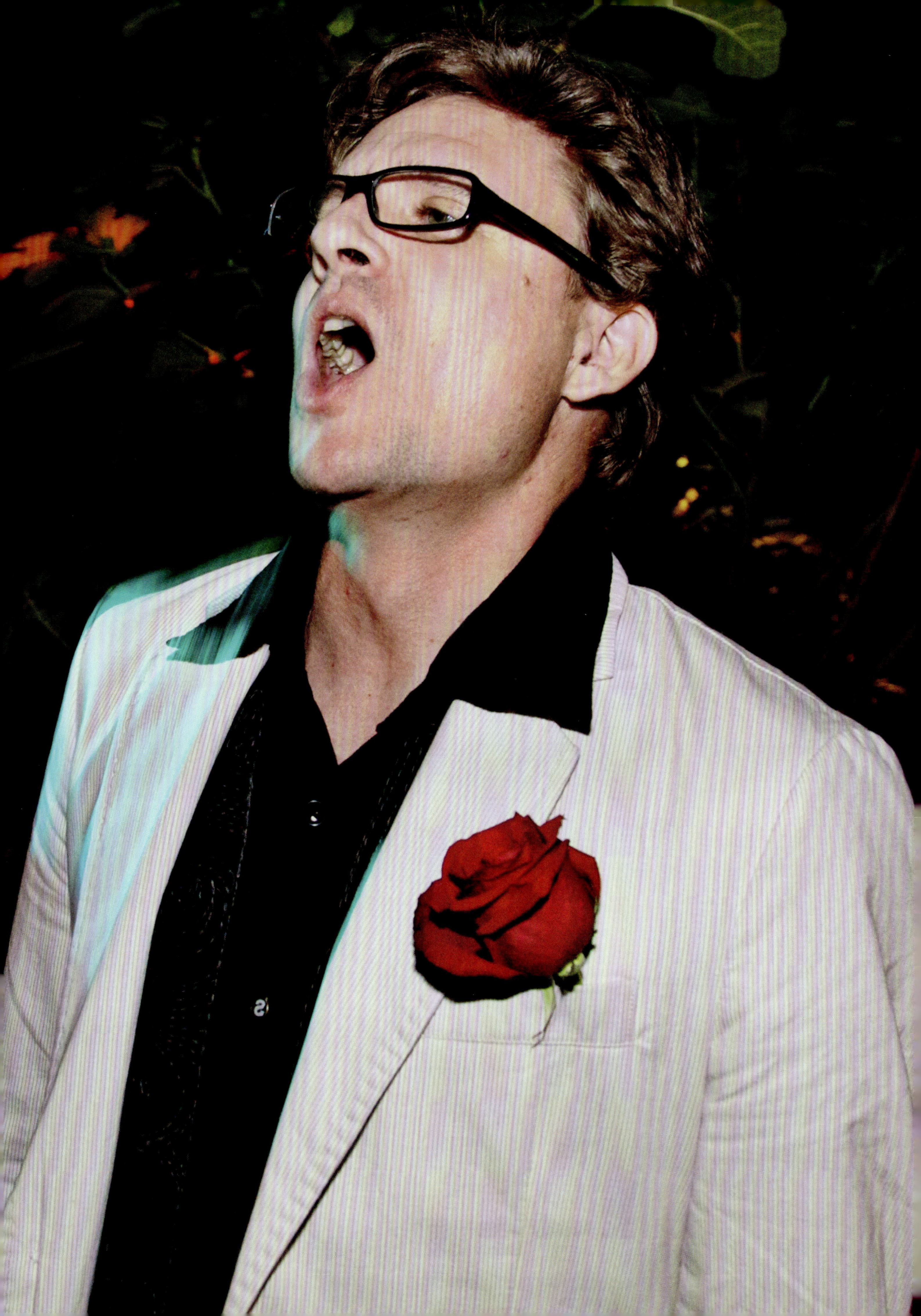

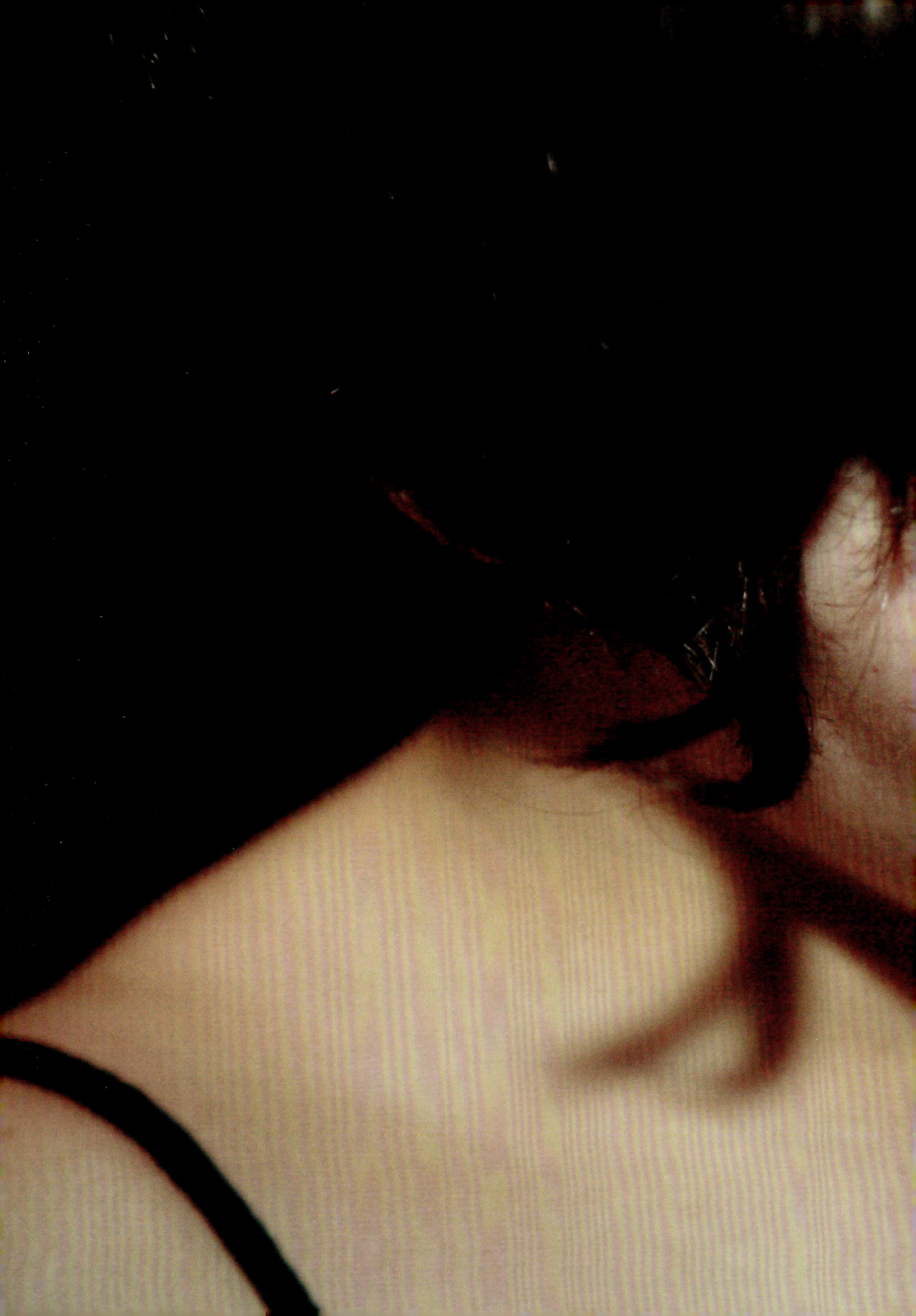

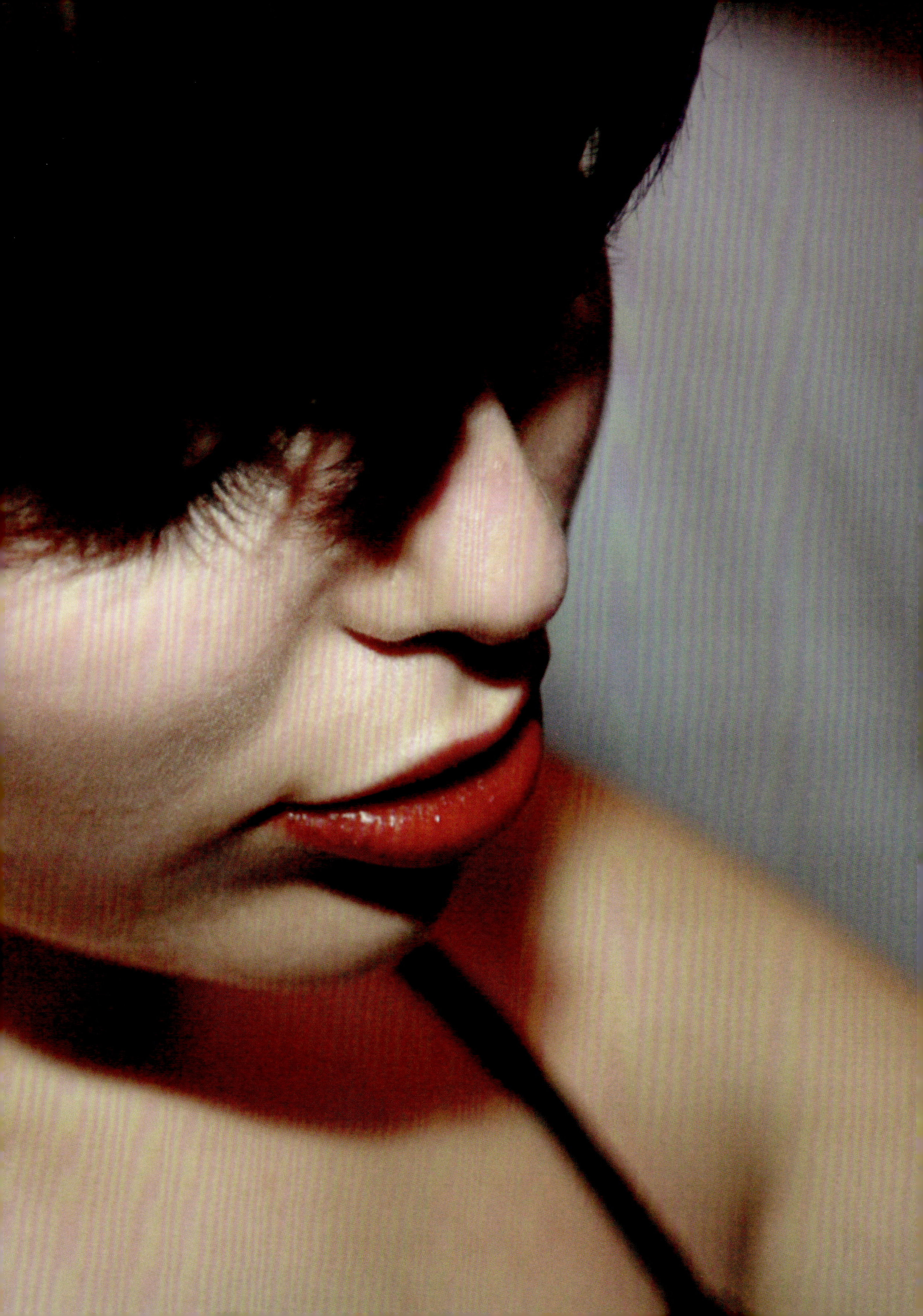

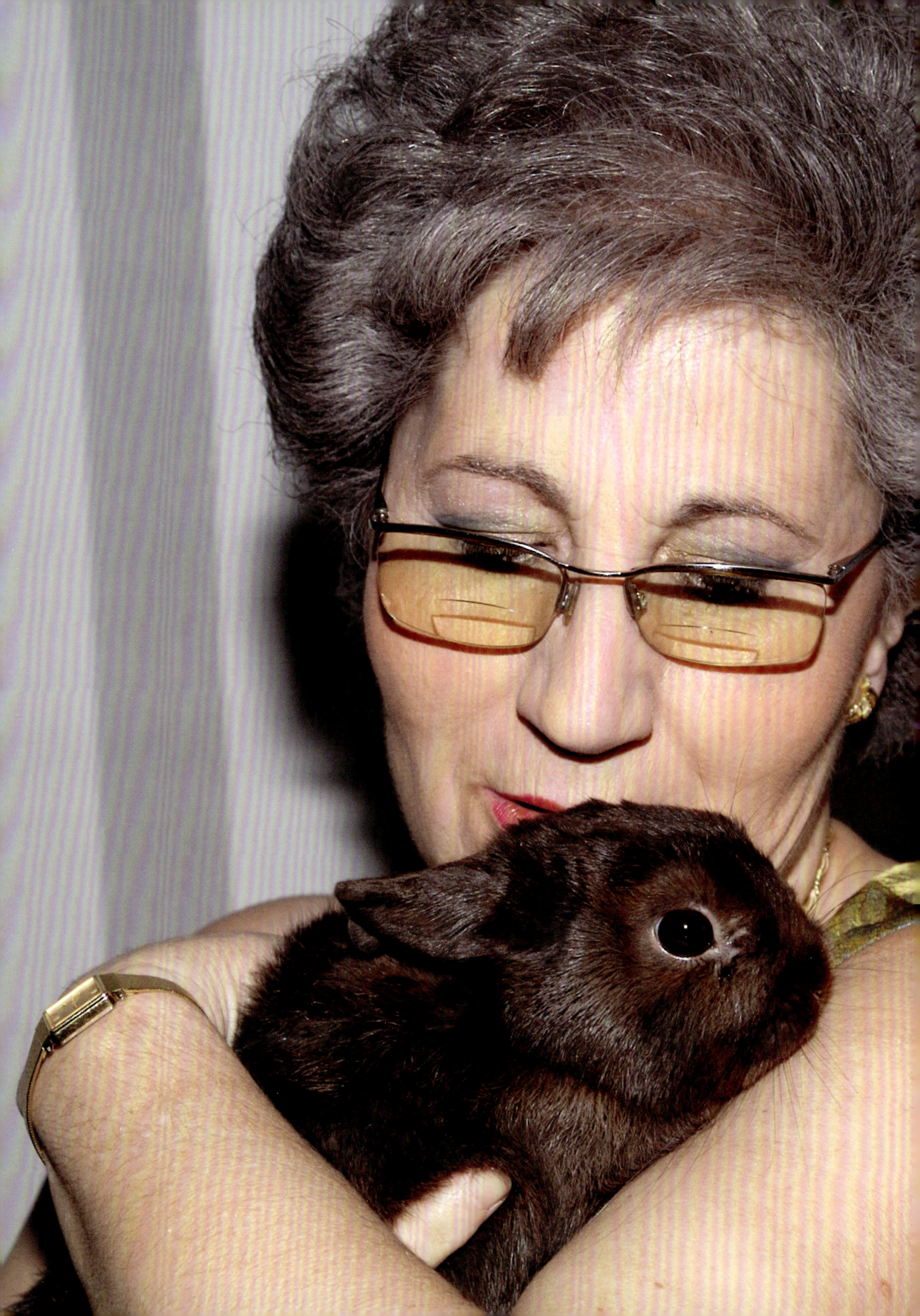

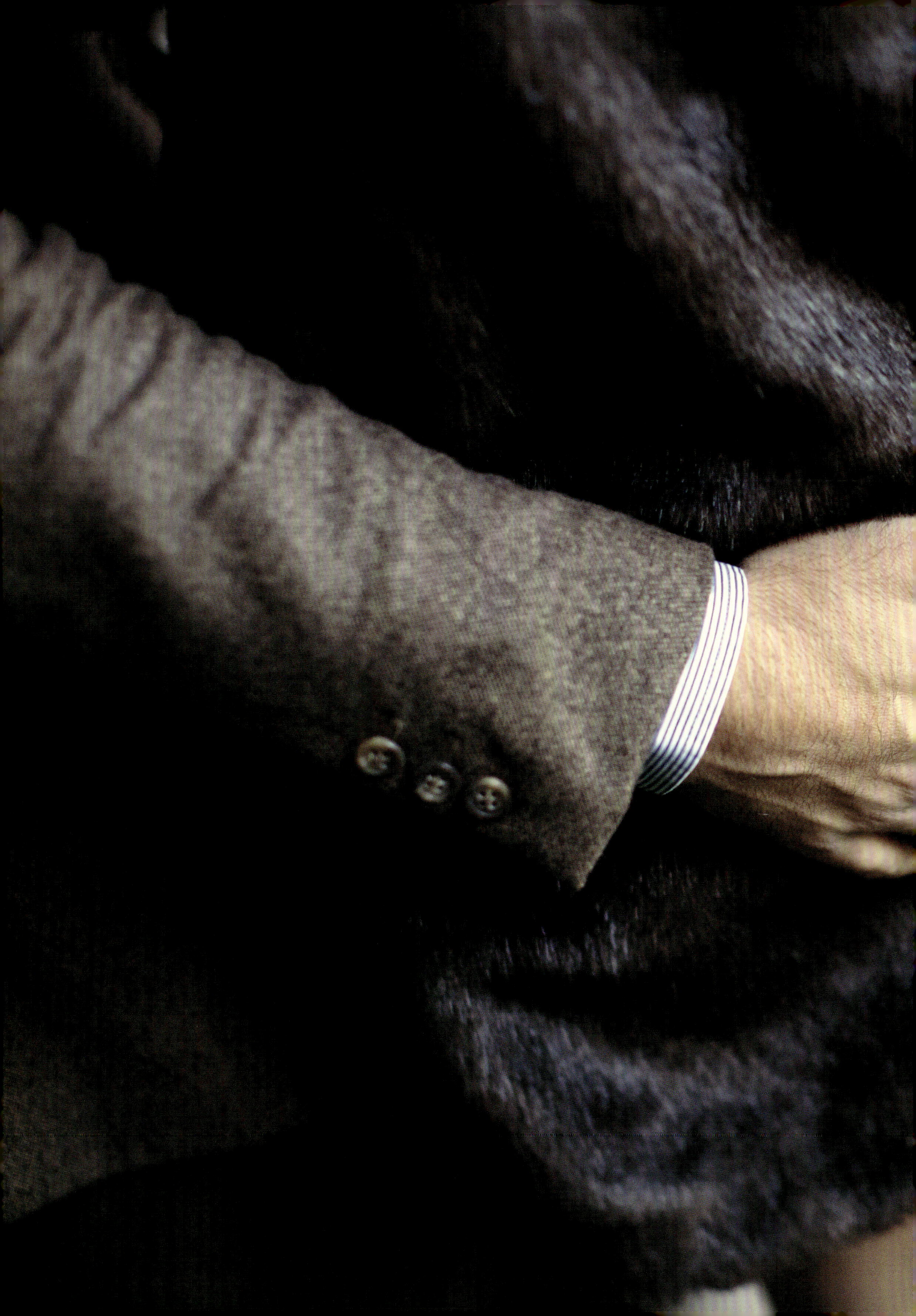

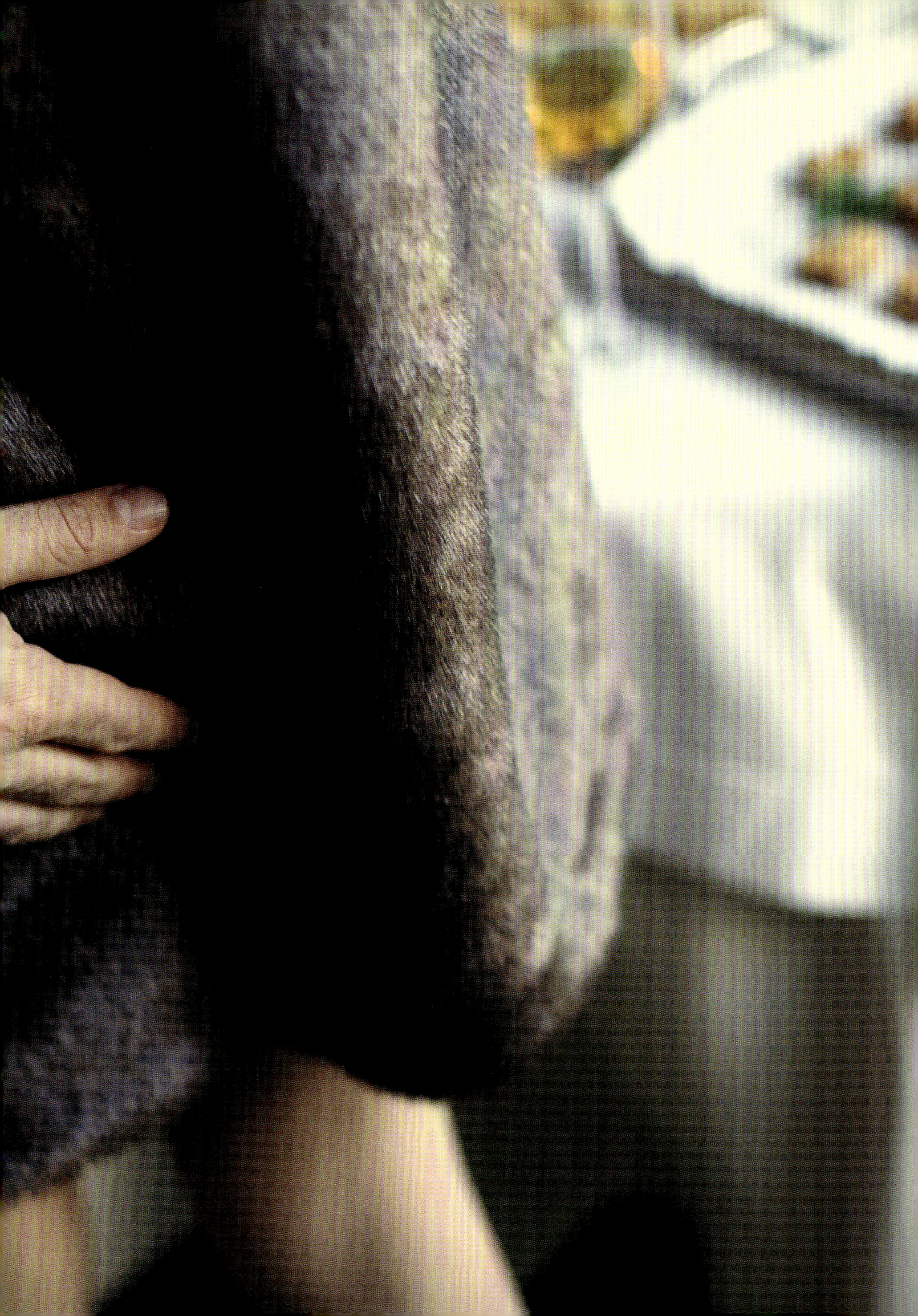

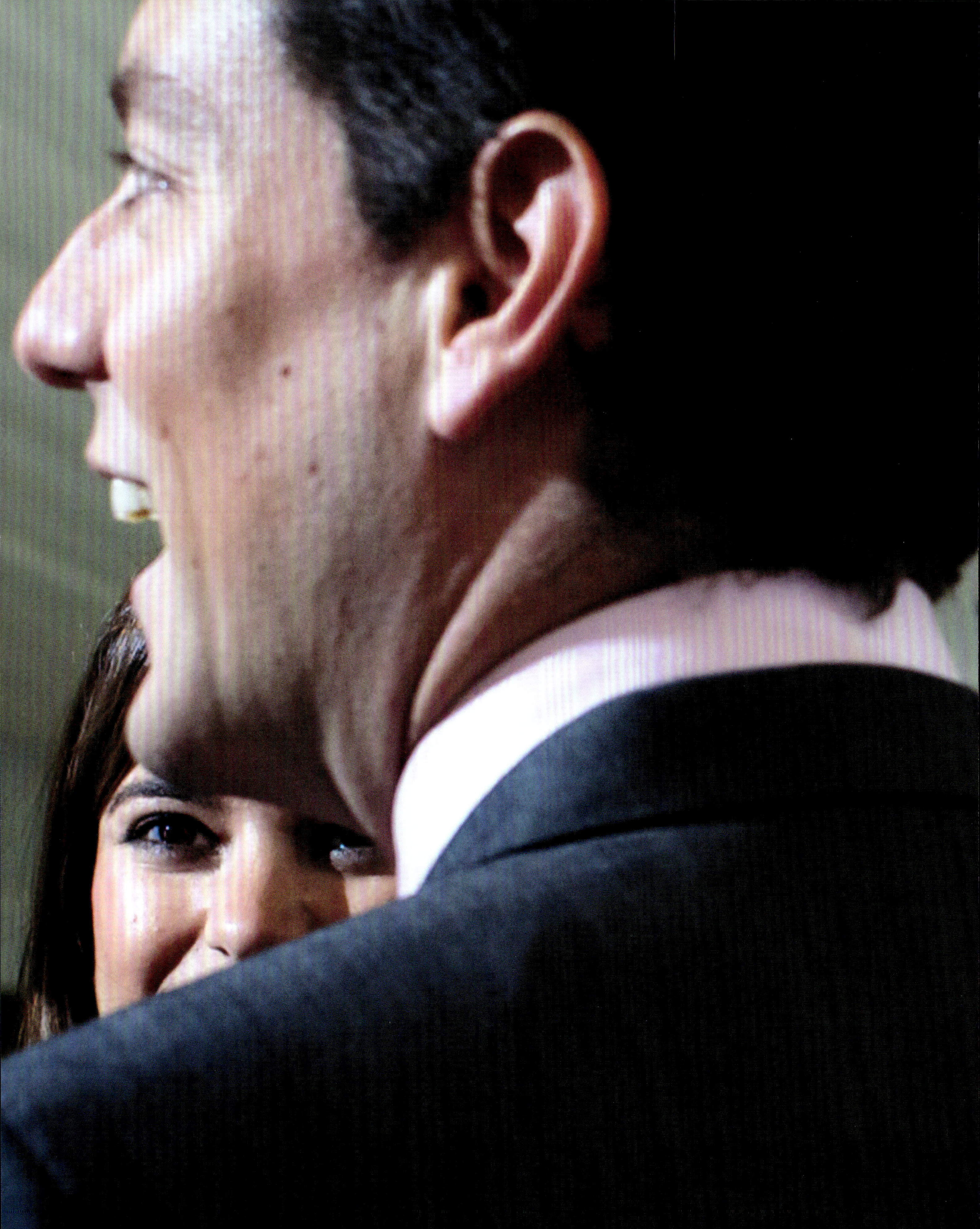

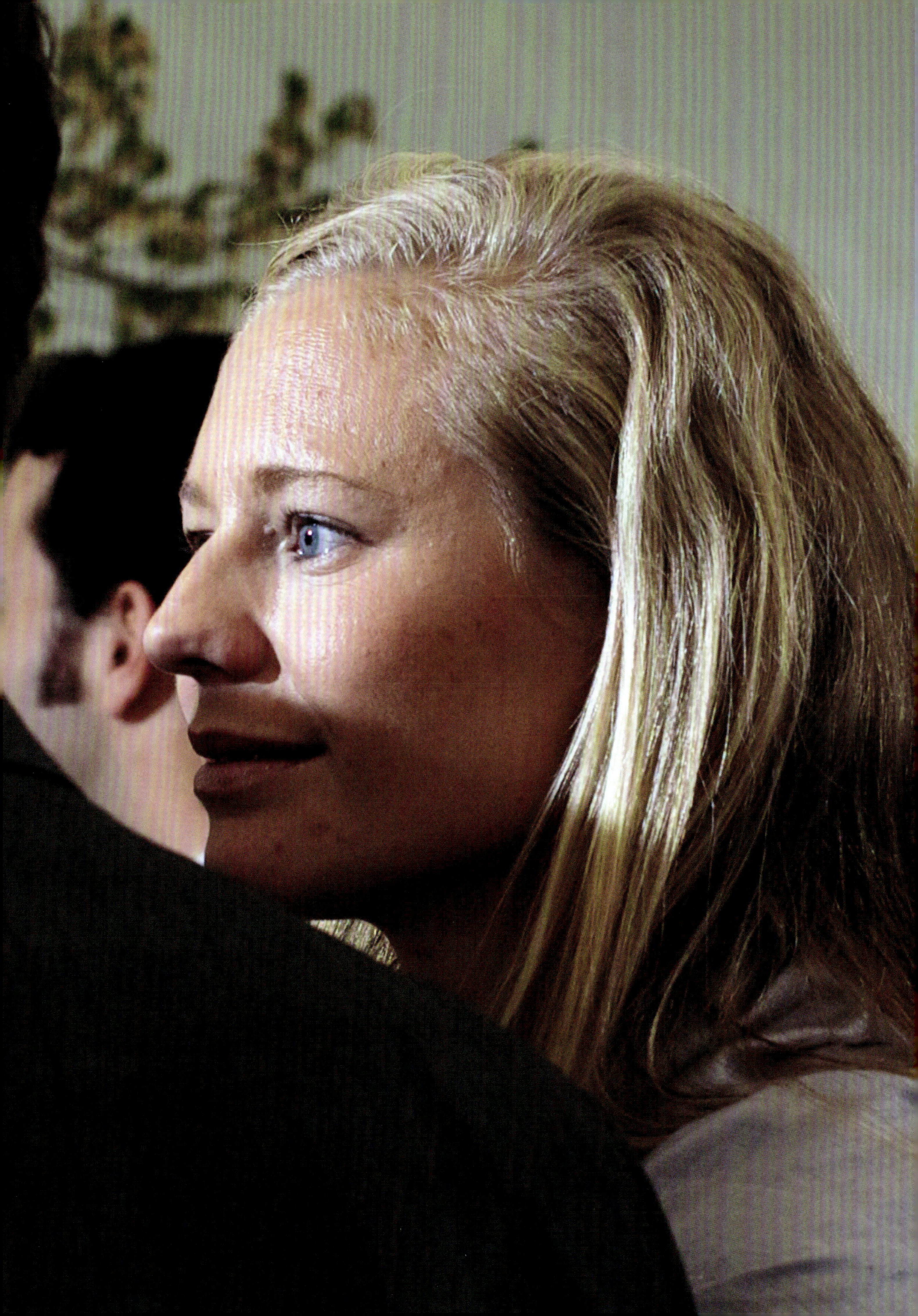

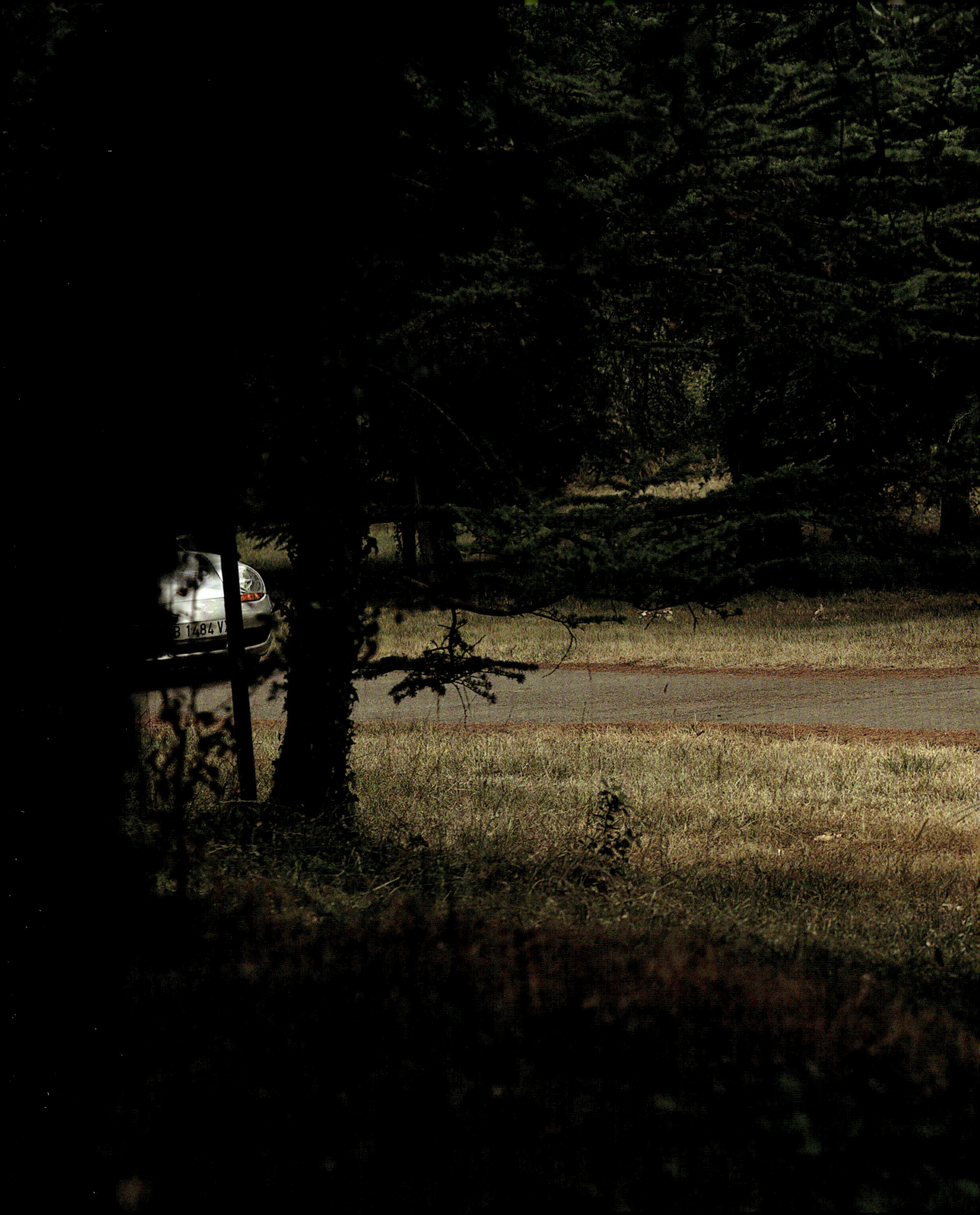

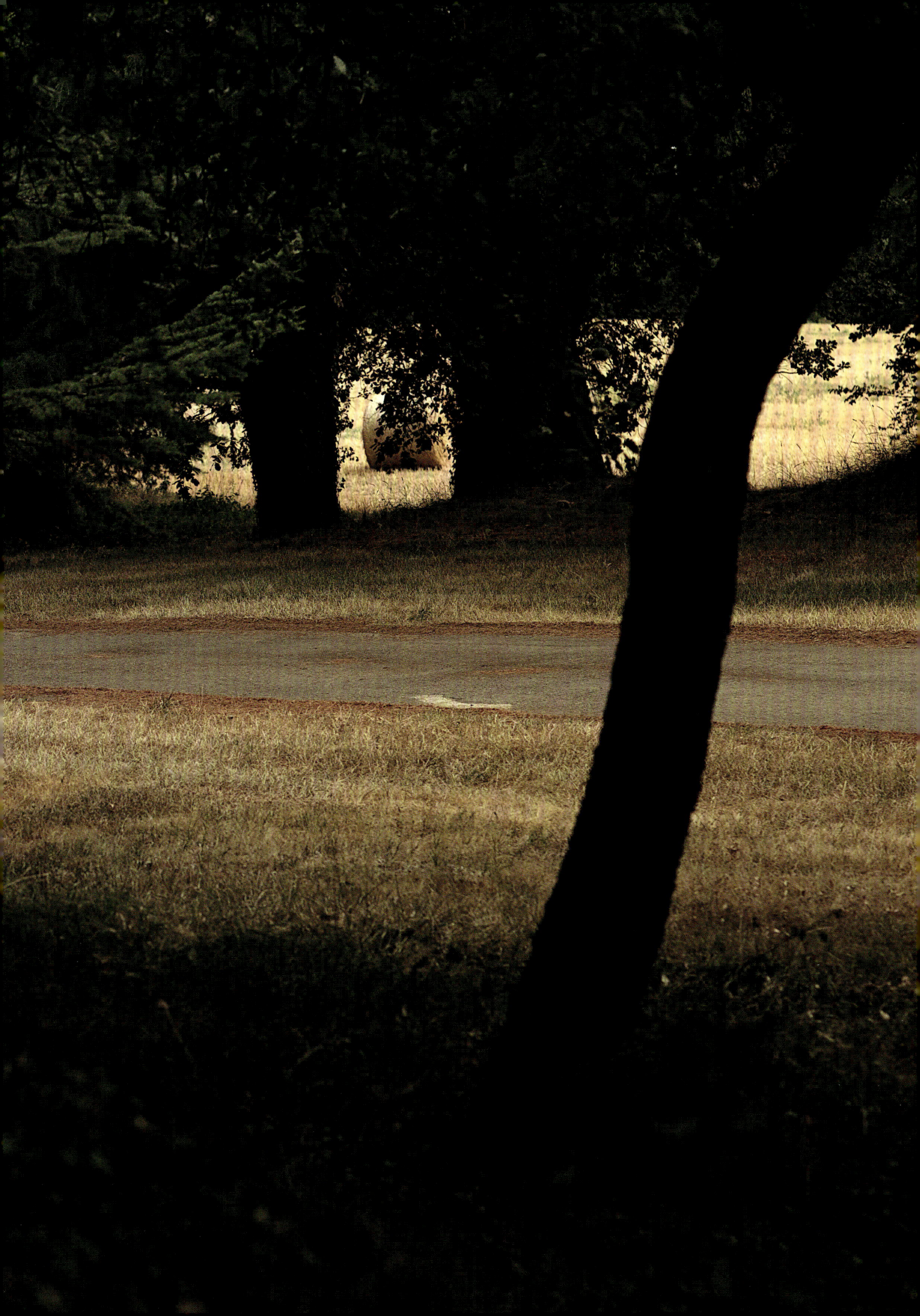

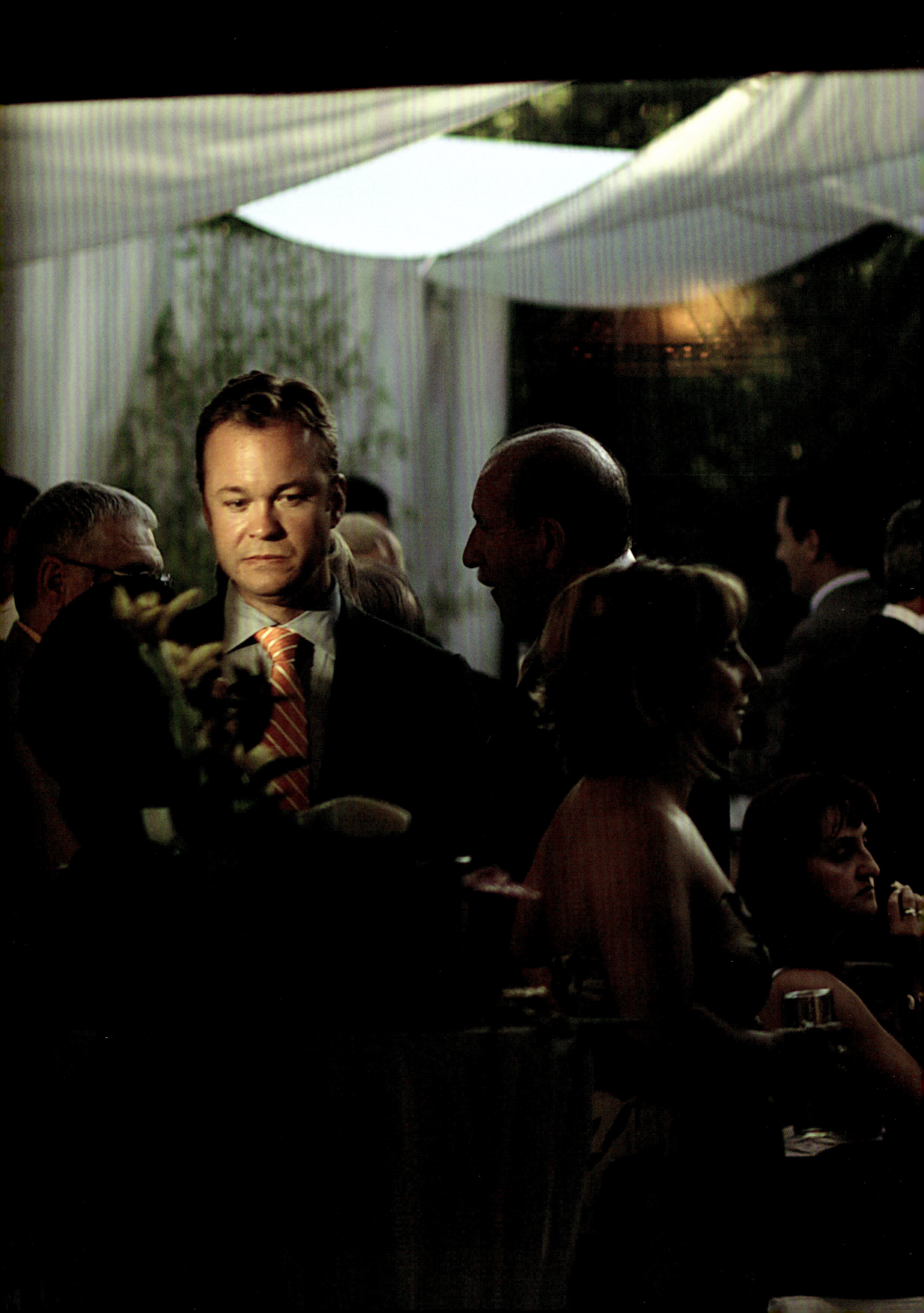

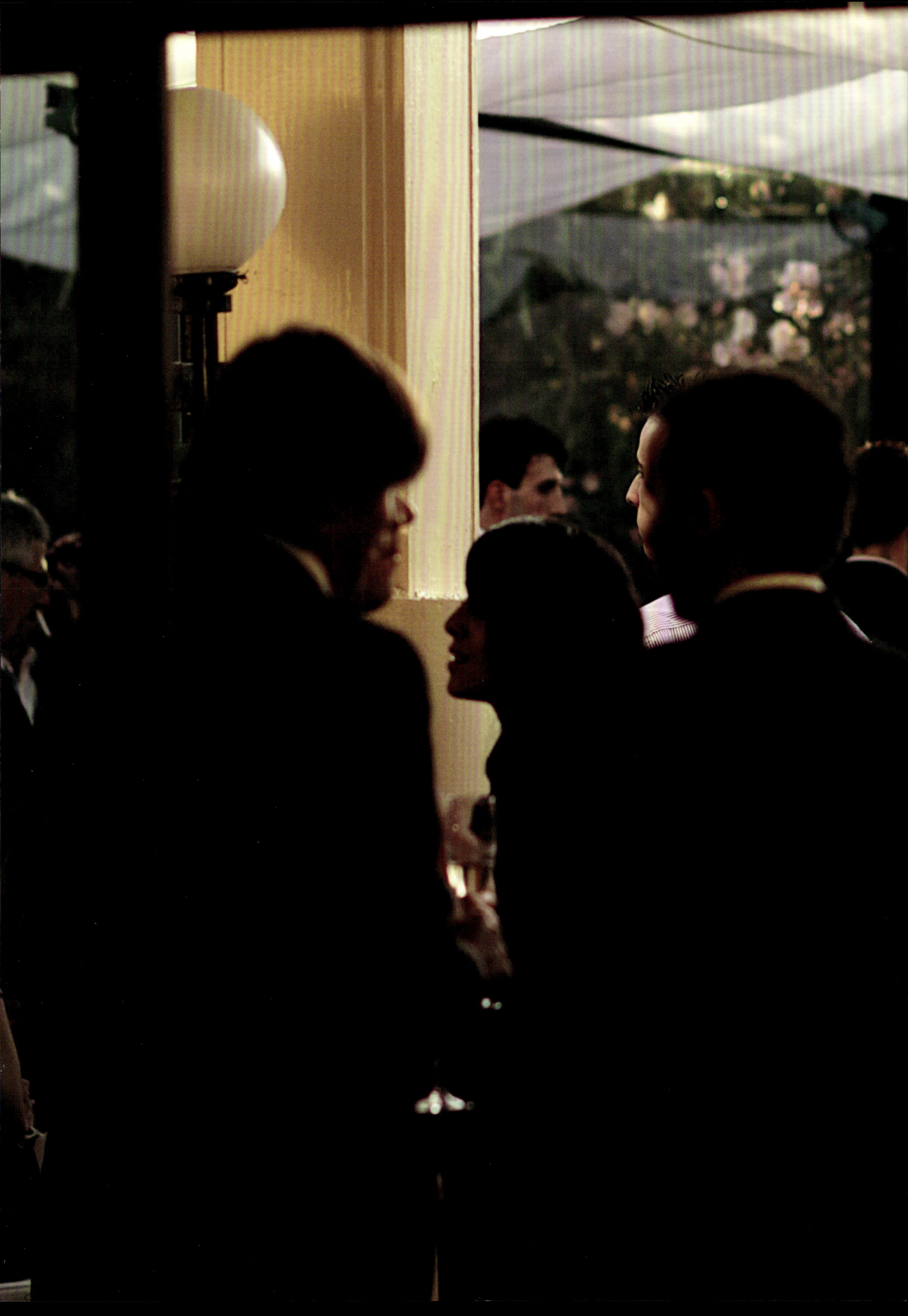

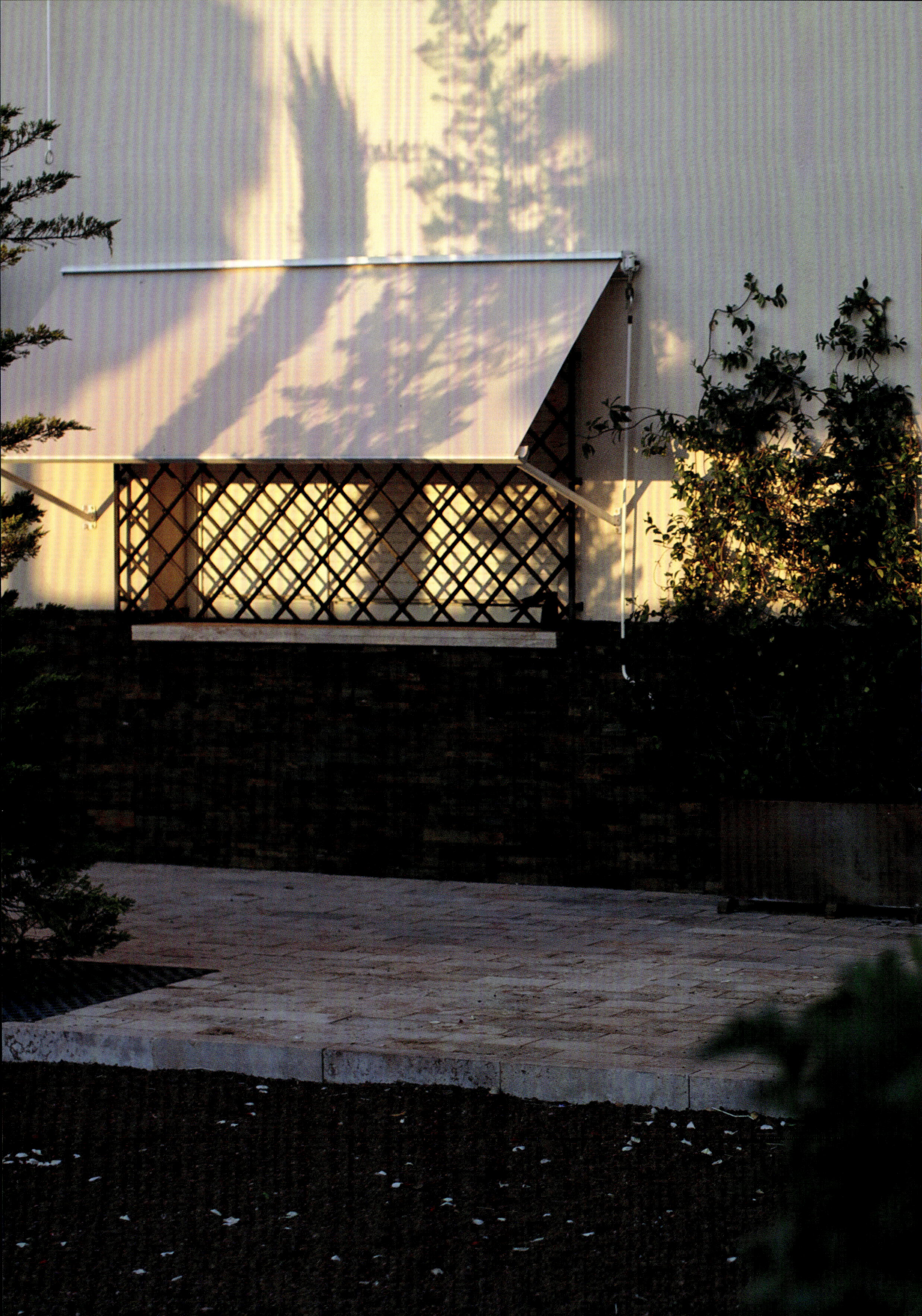

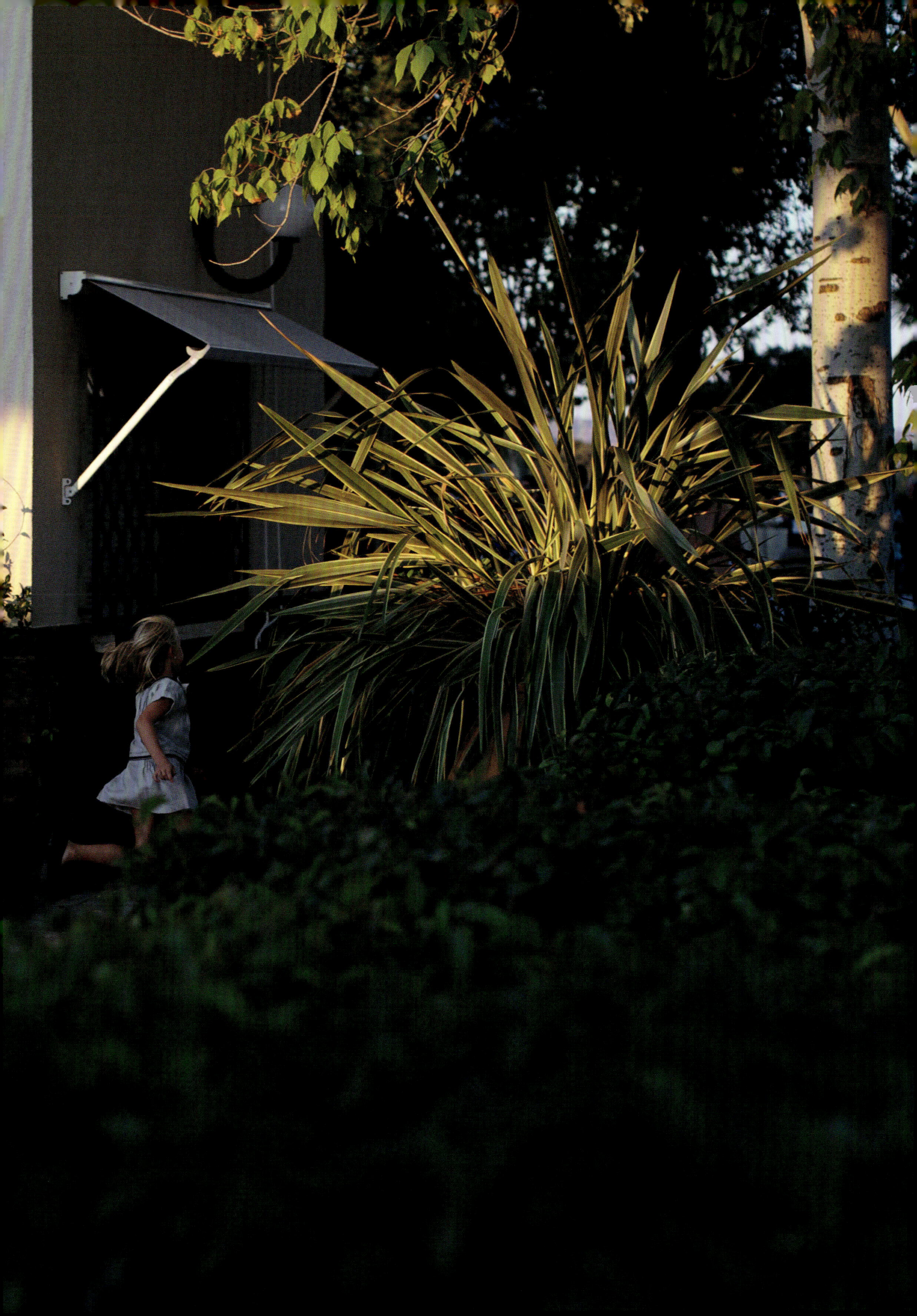

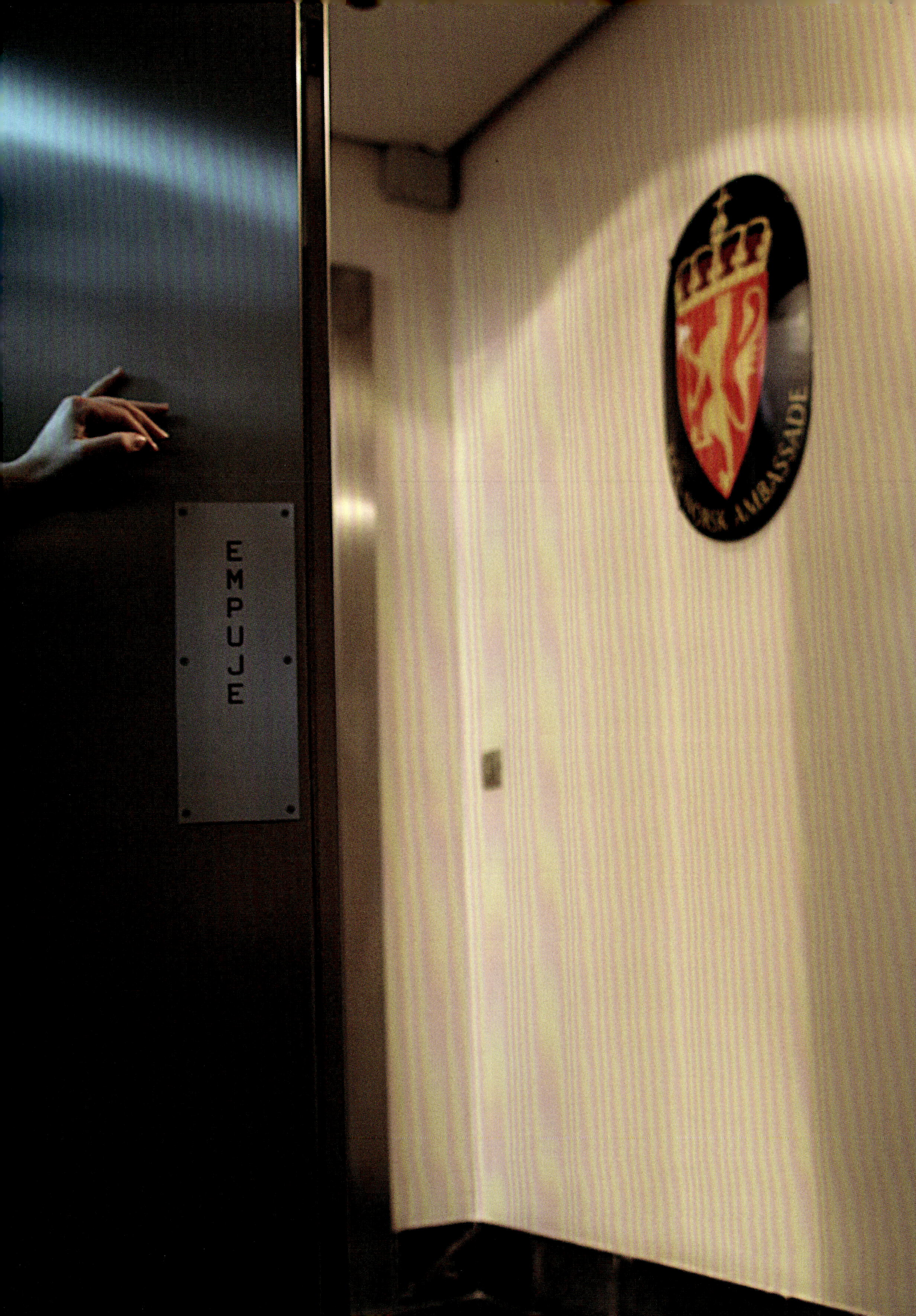
EMPUJE
NORSK AMBASSADE

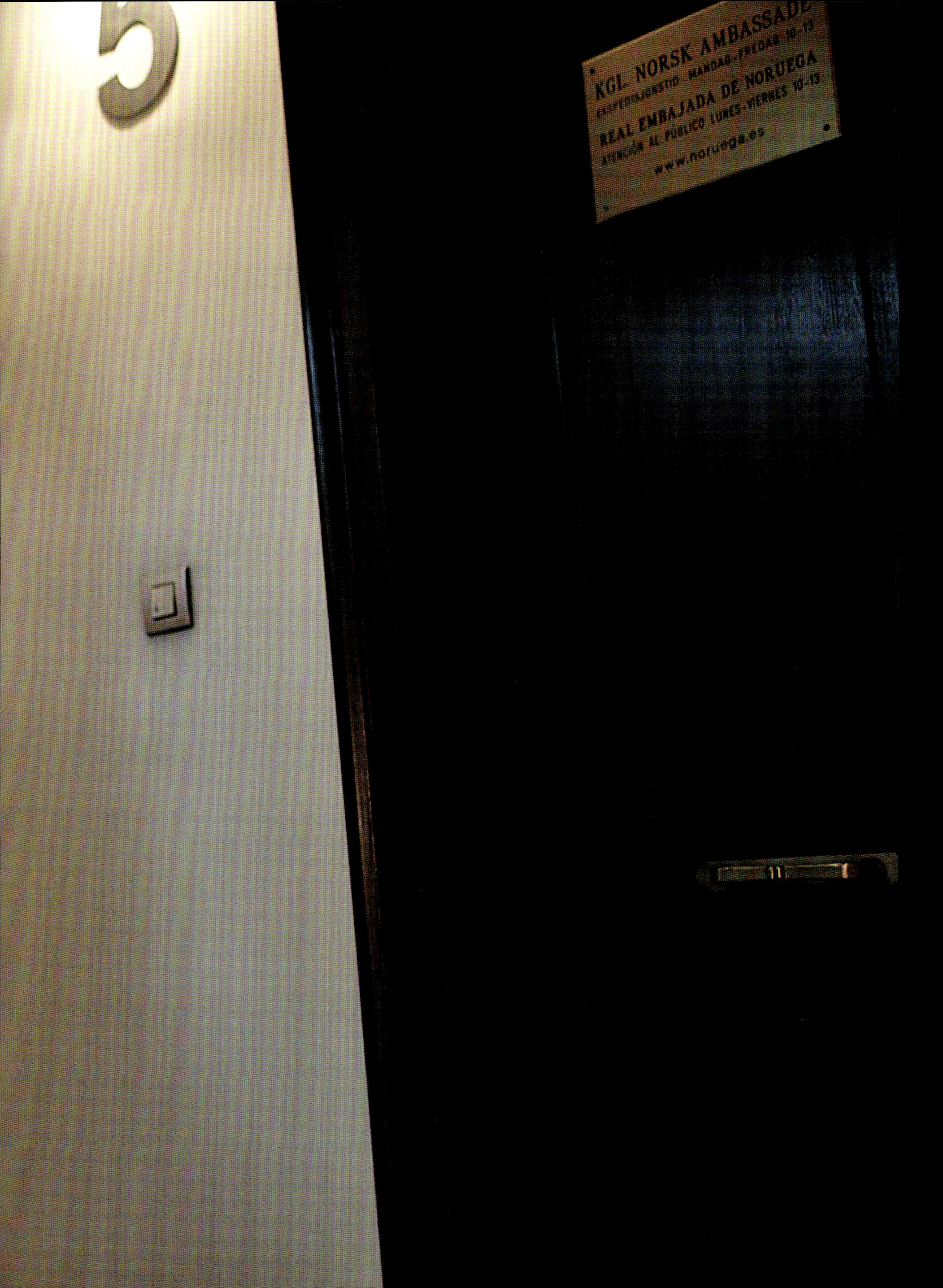

5
KGL. NORSK AMBASSADE
EKSPEDISJONSTID: MANDAG-FREDAG 10-13
REAL EMBAJADA DE NORUEGA
ATENCIÓN AL PÚBLICO LUNES-VIERNES 10-13
www.noruega.es

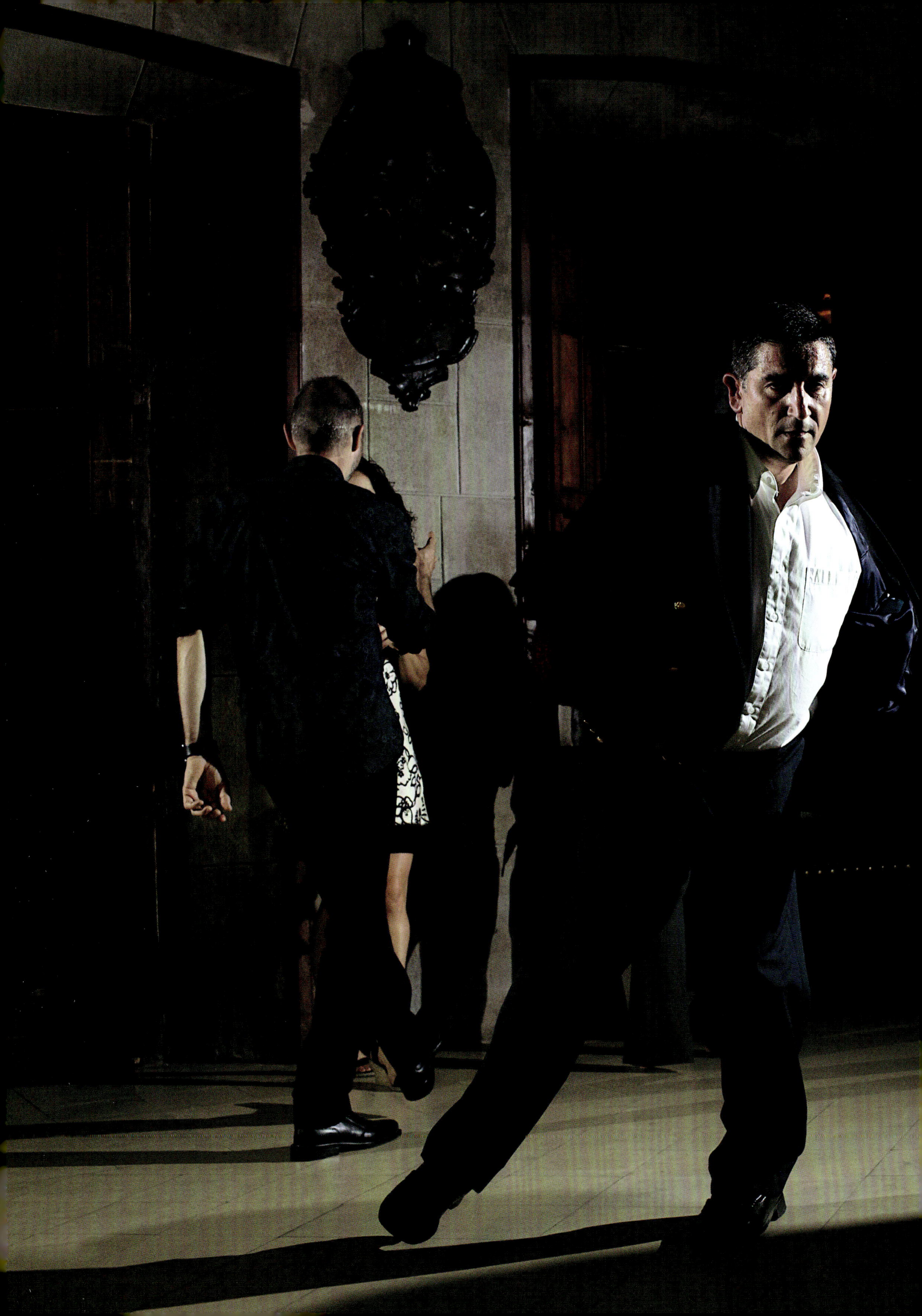

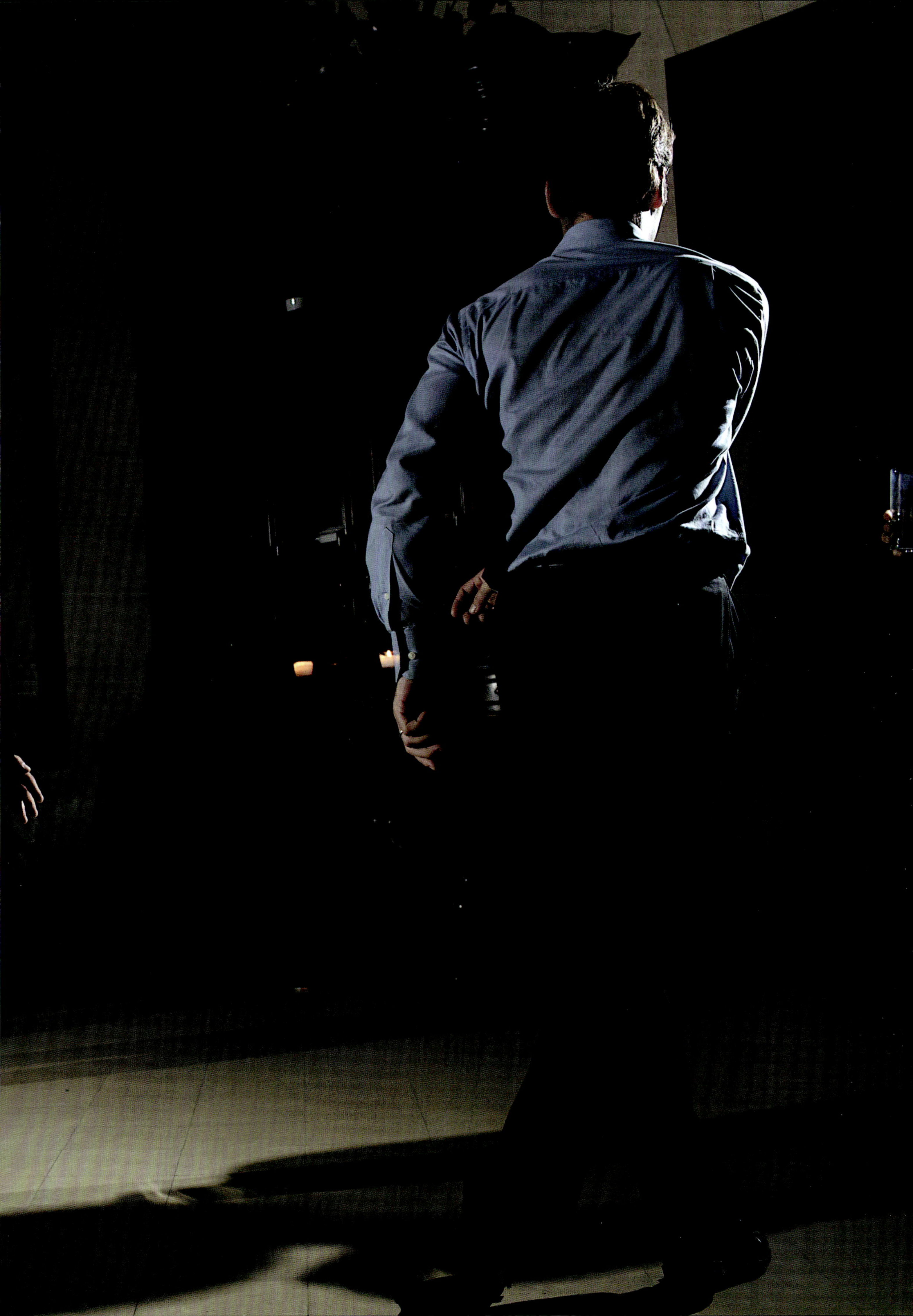

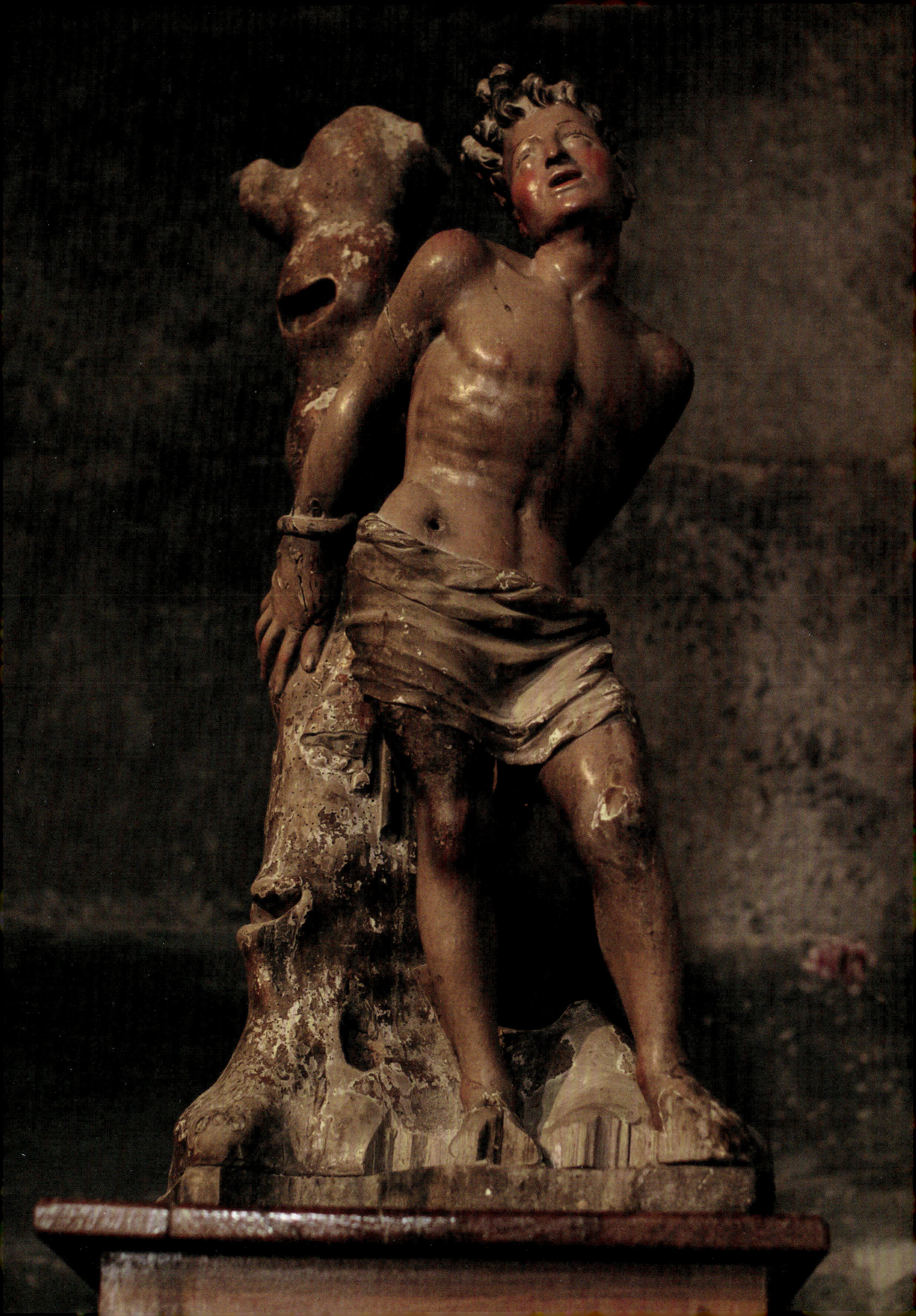

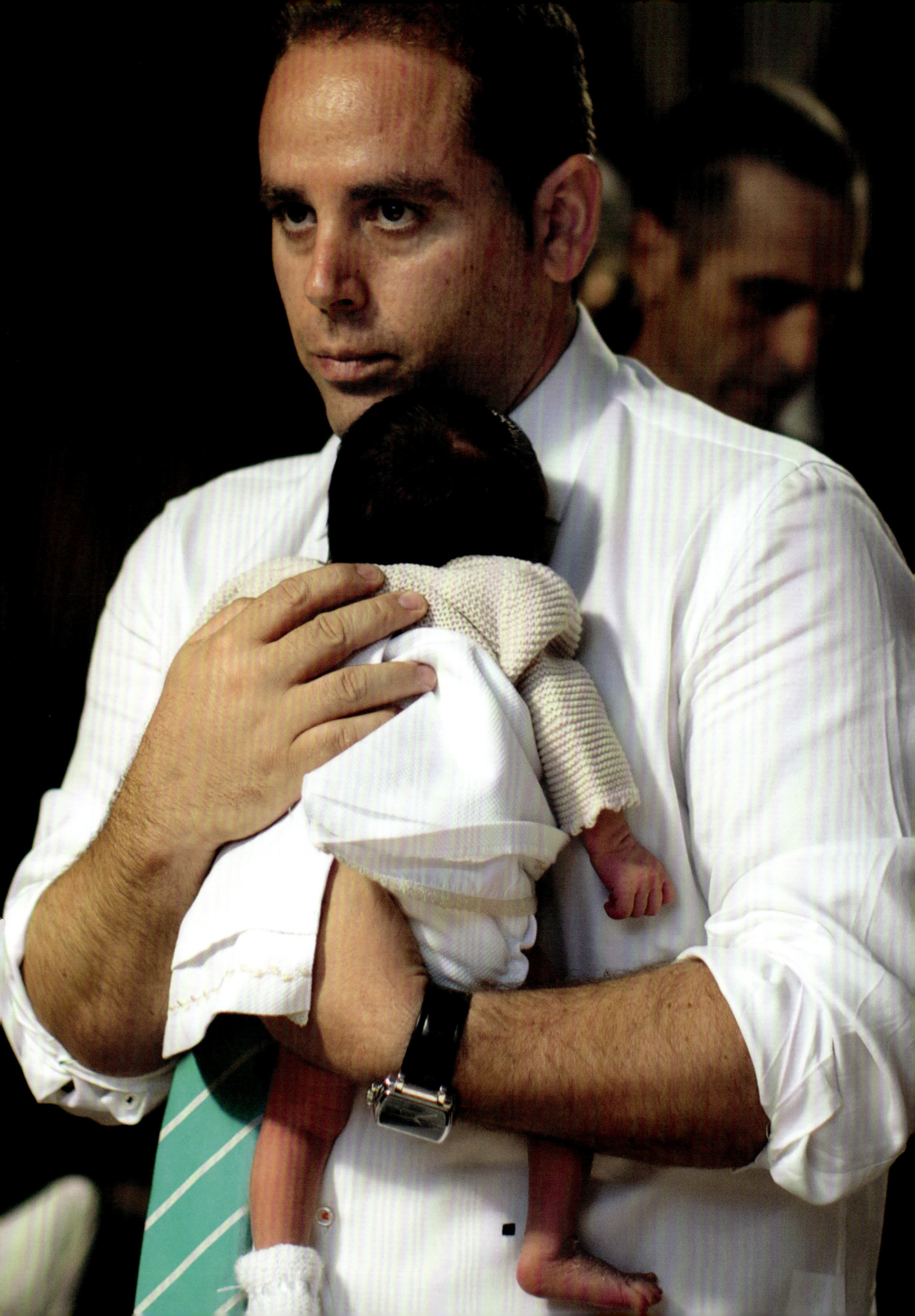

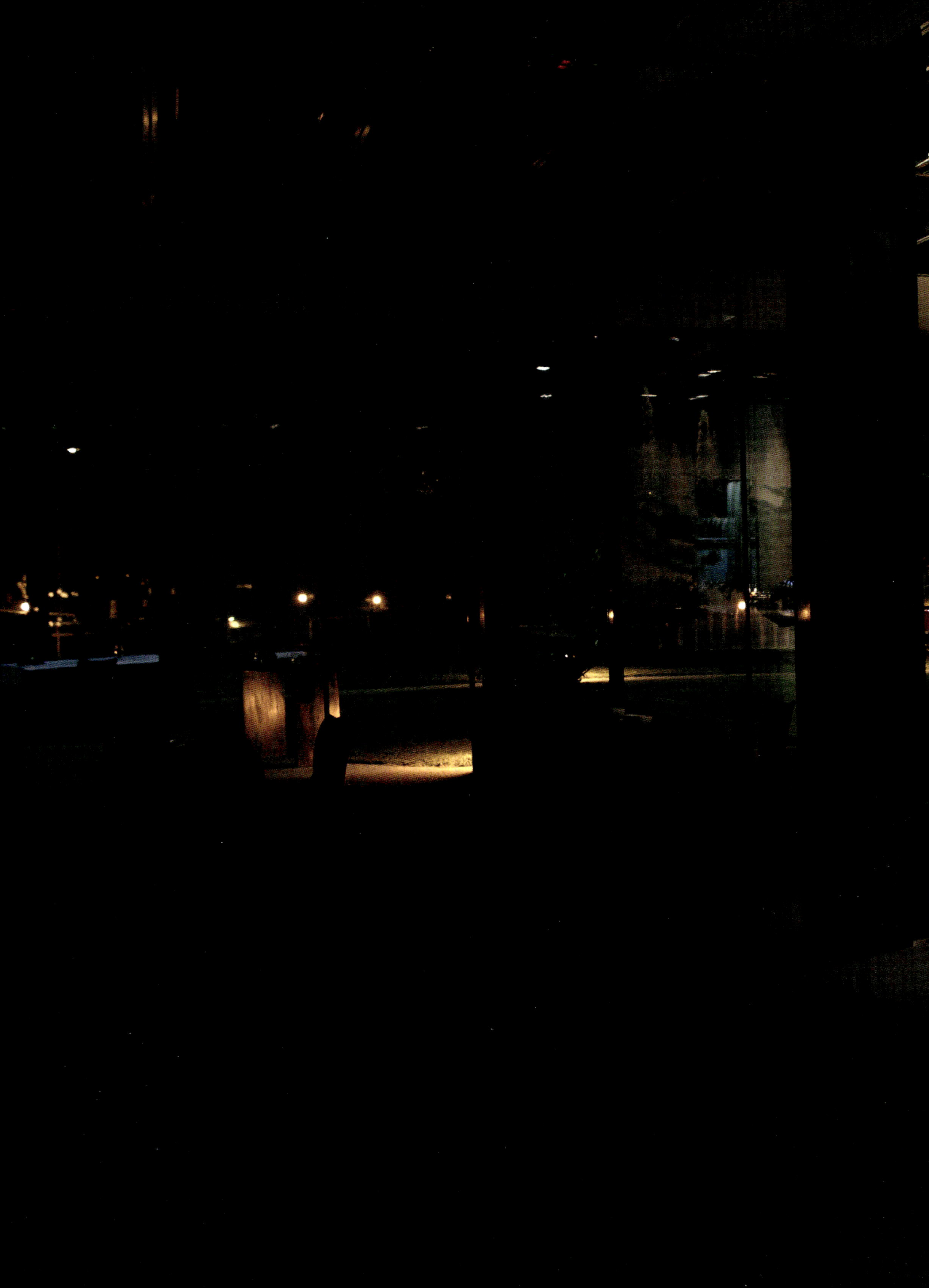

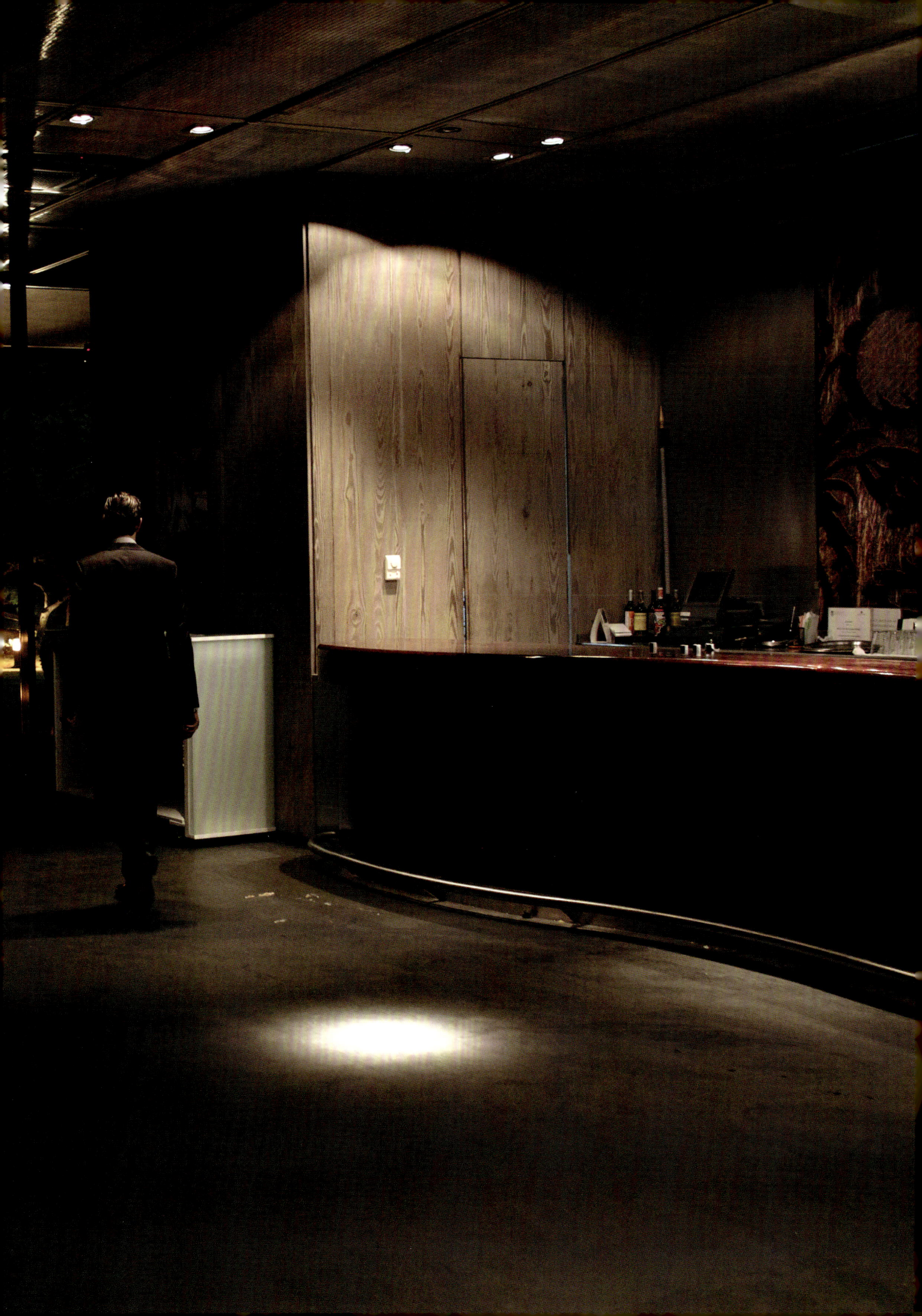

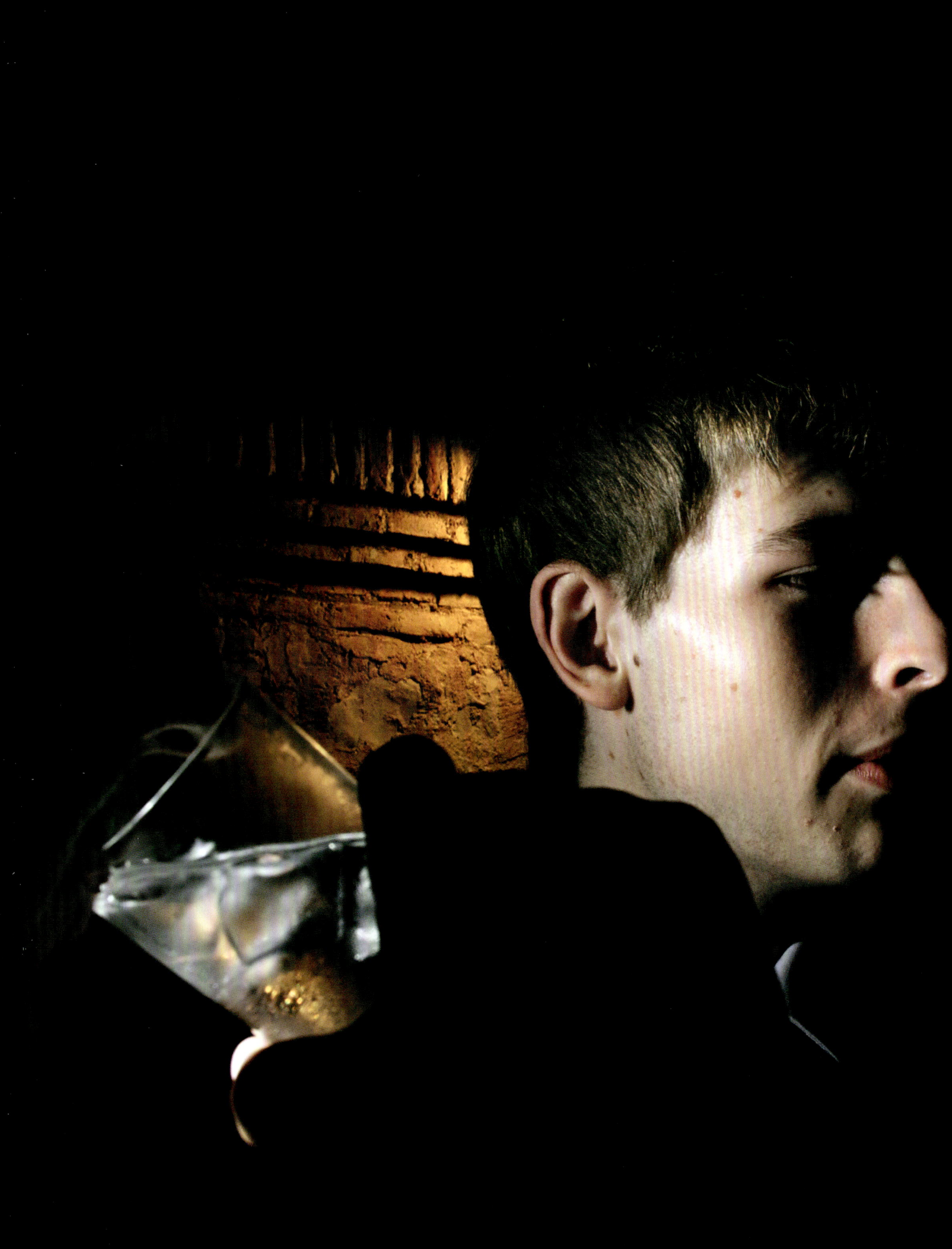

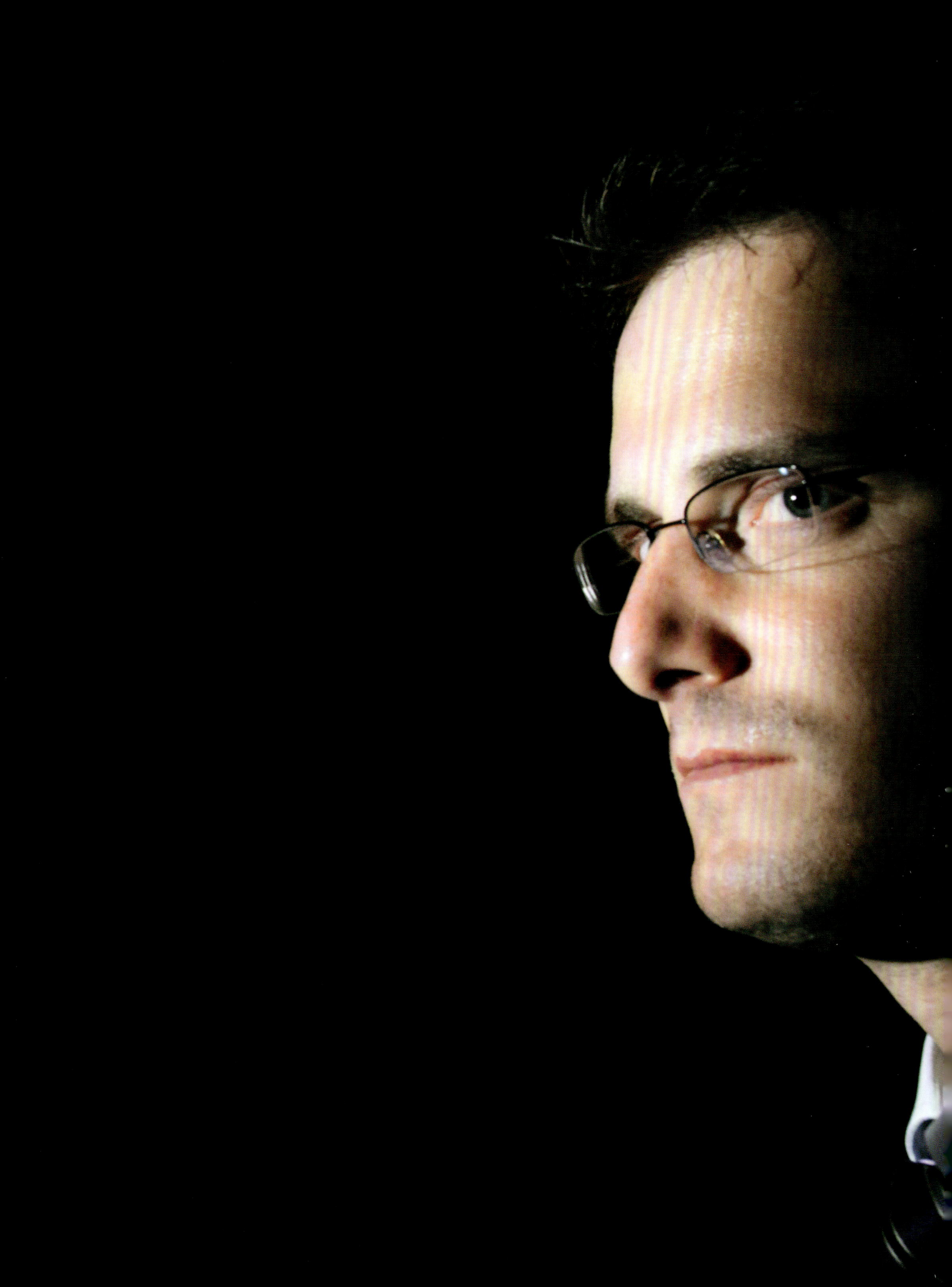

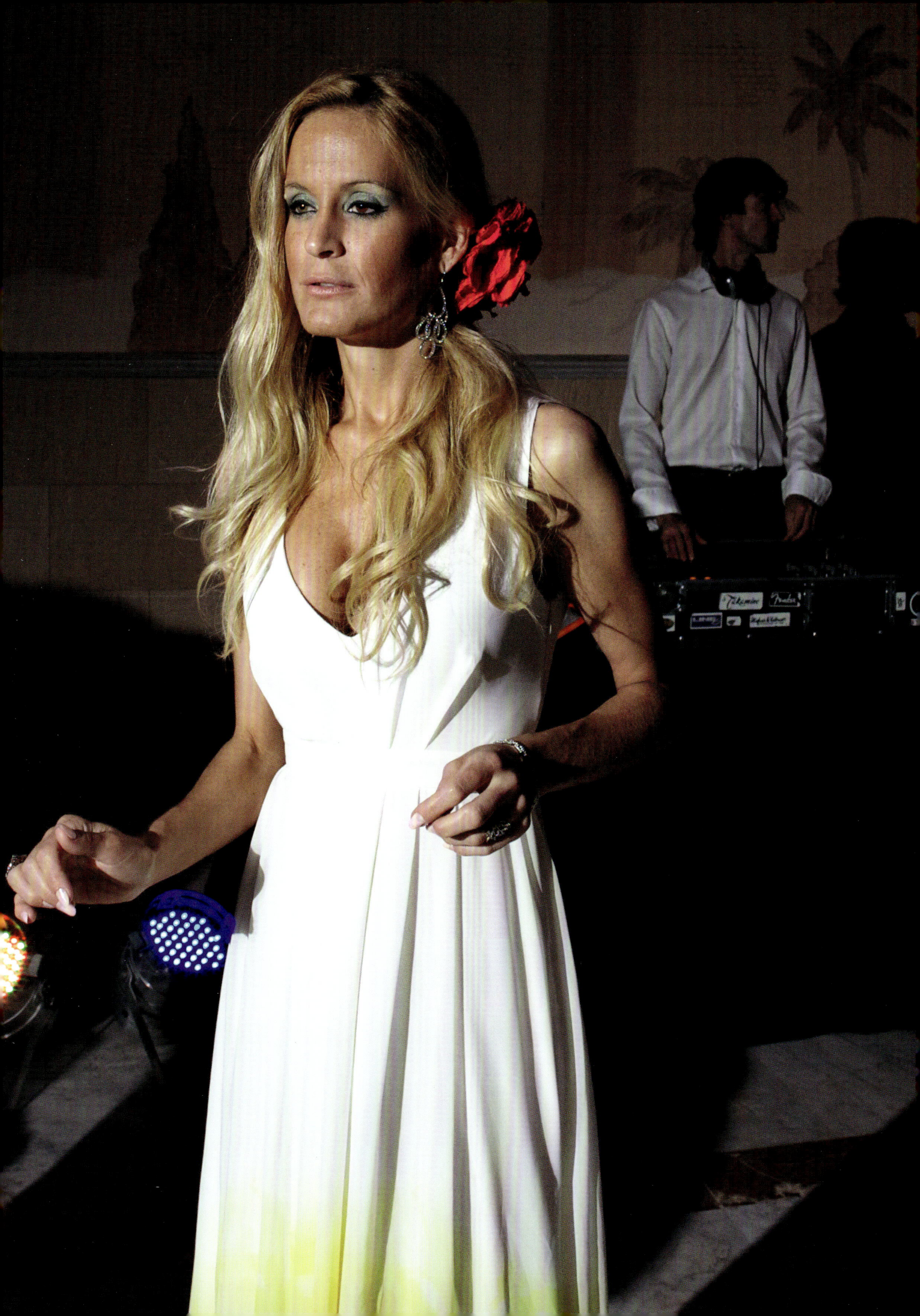

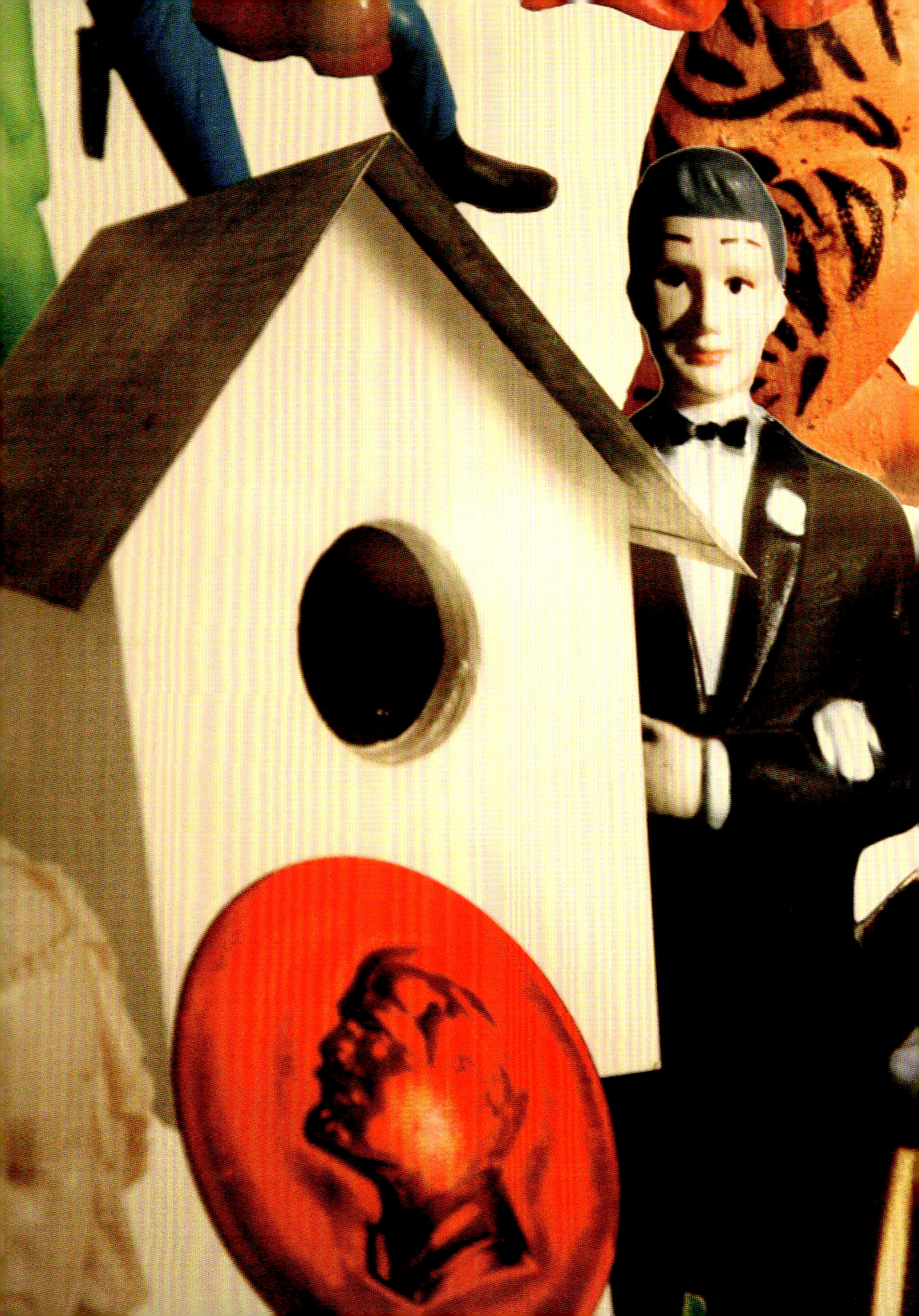

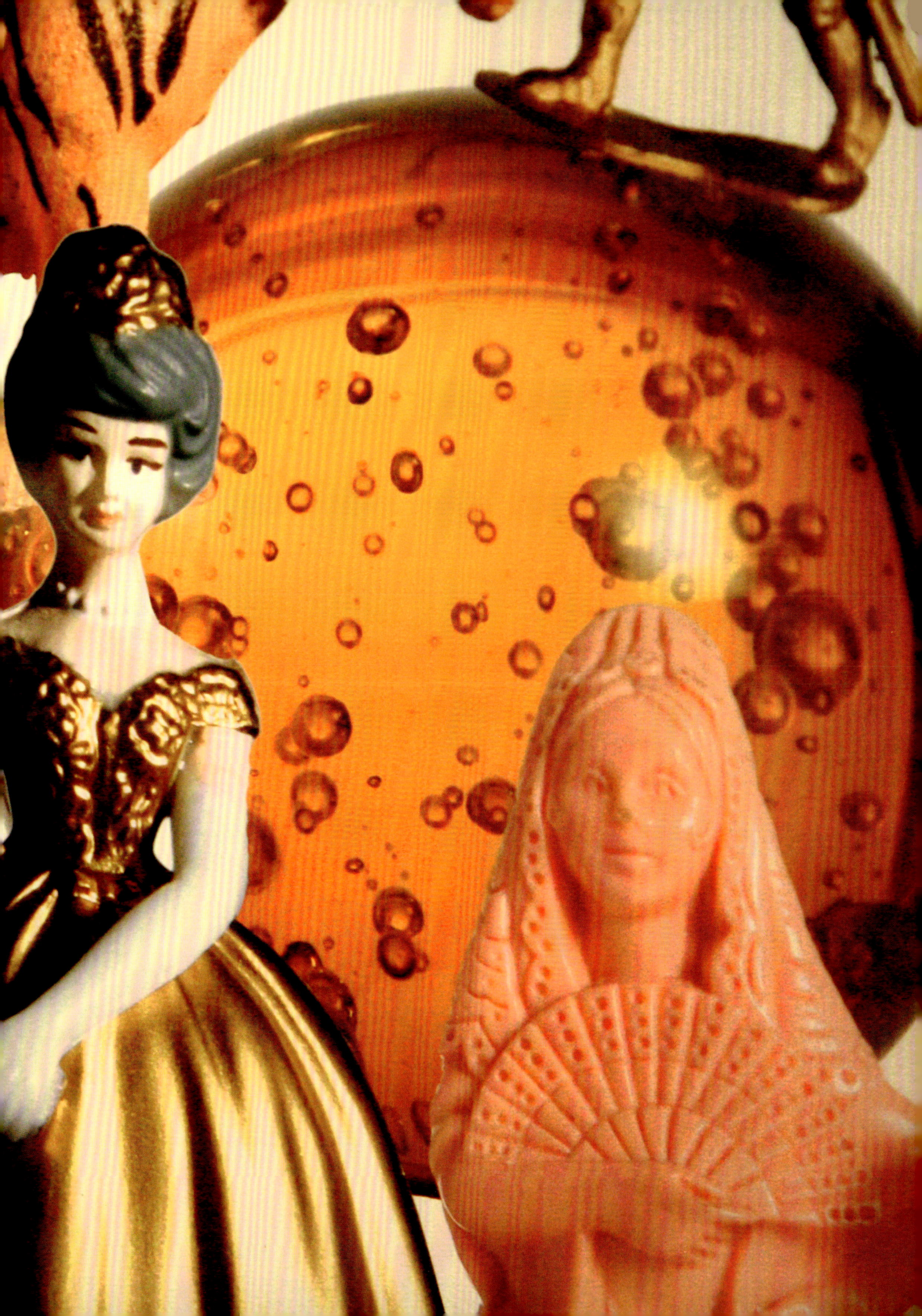

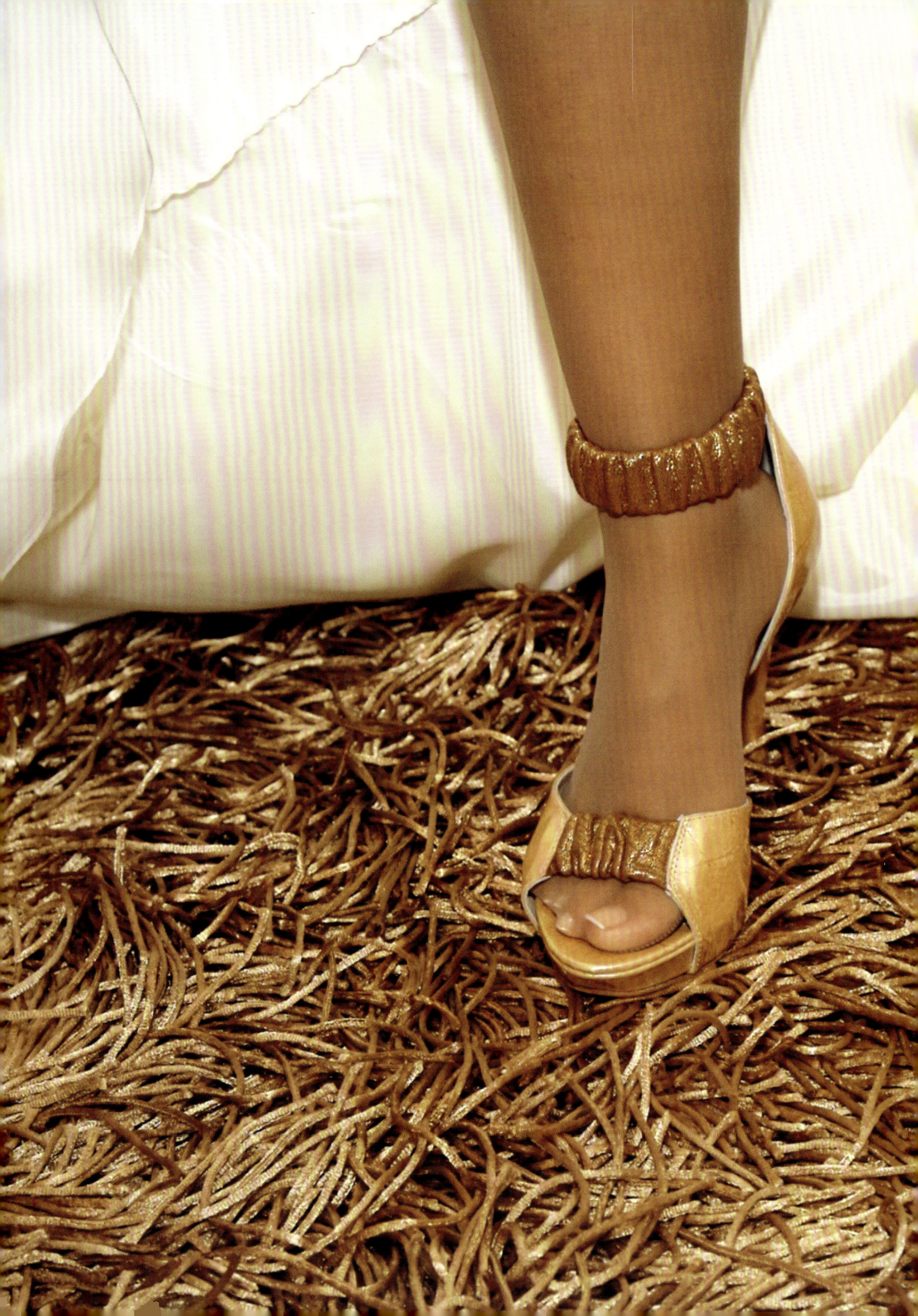

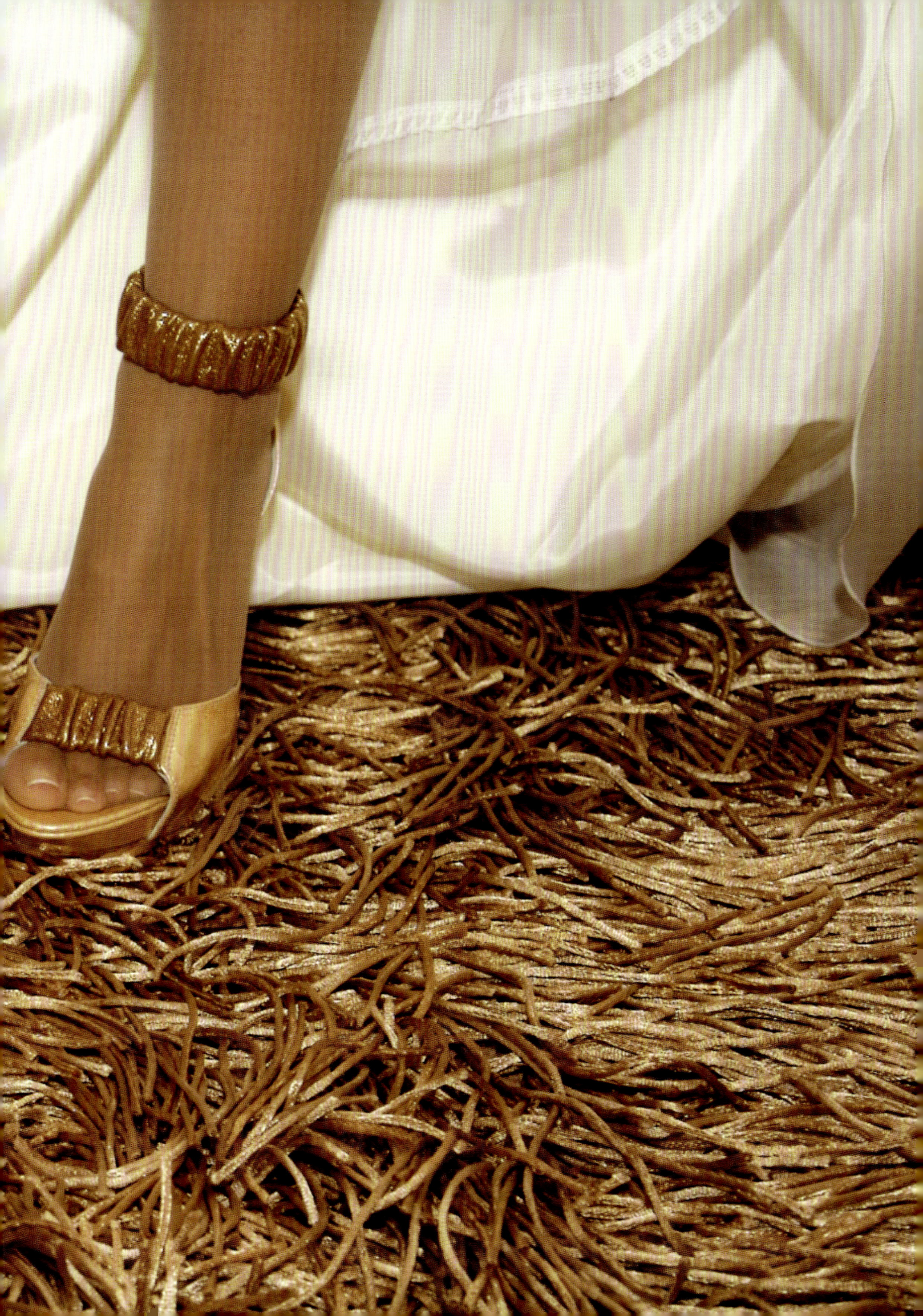

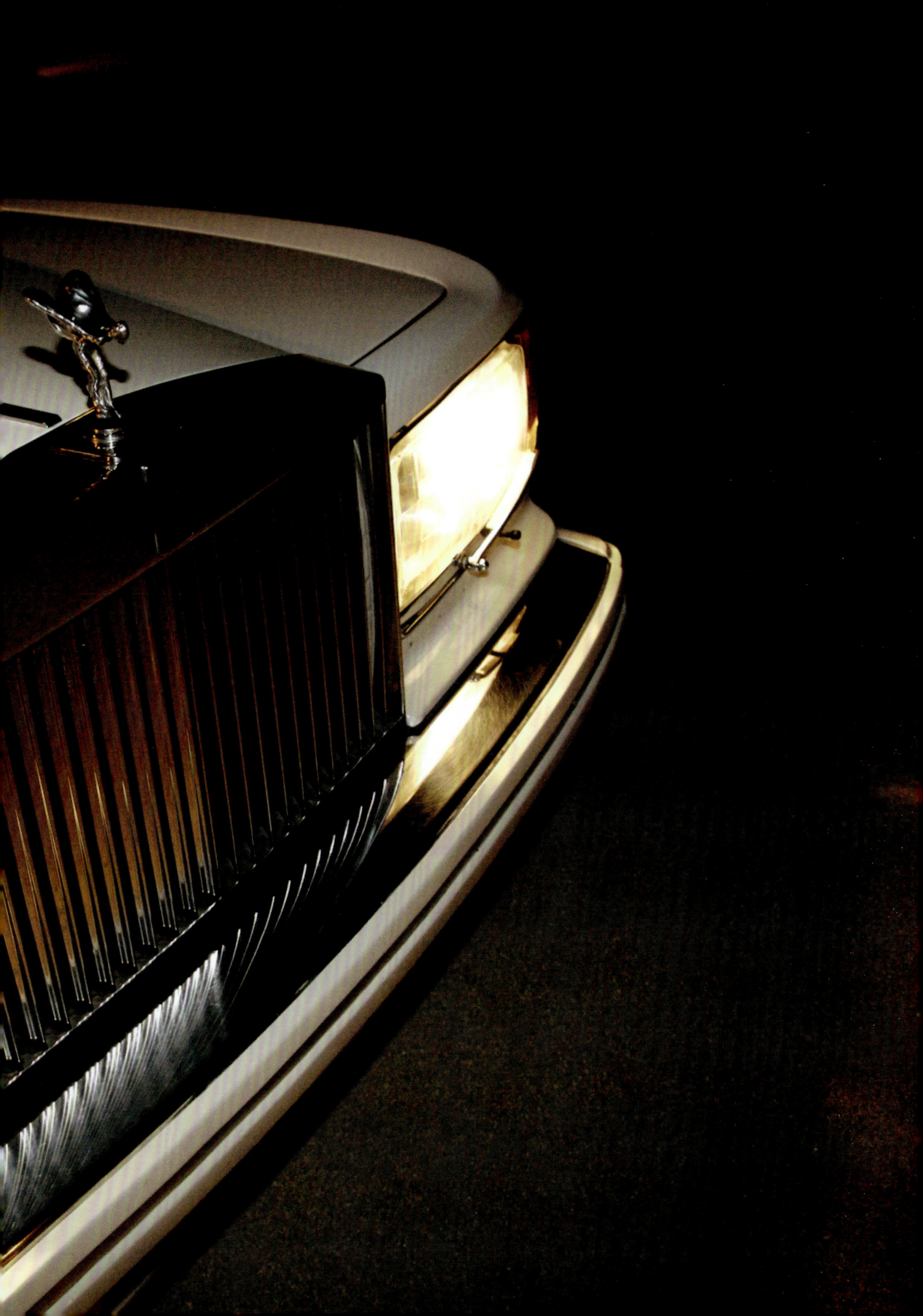

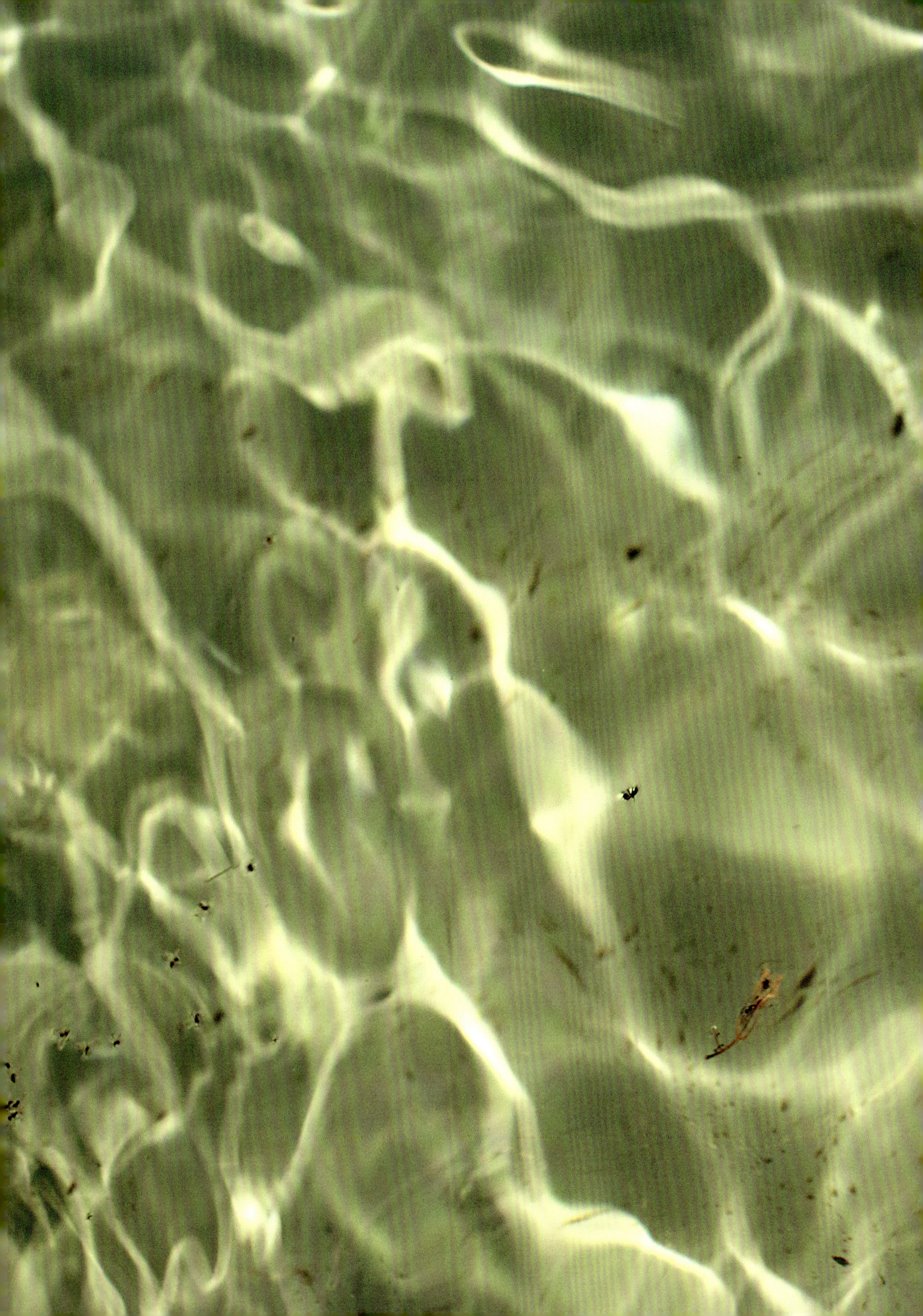

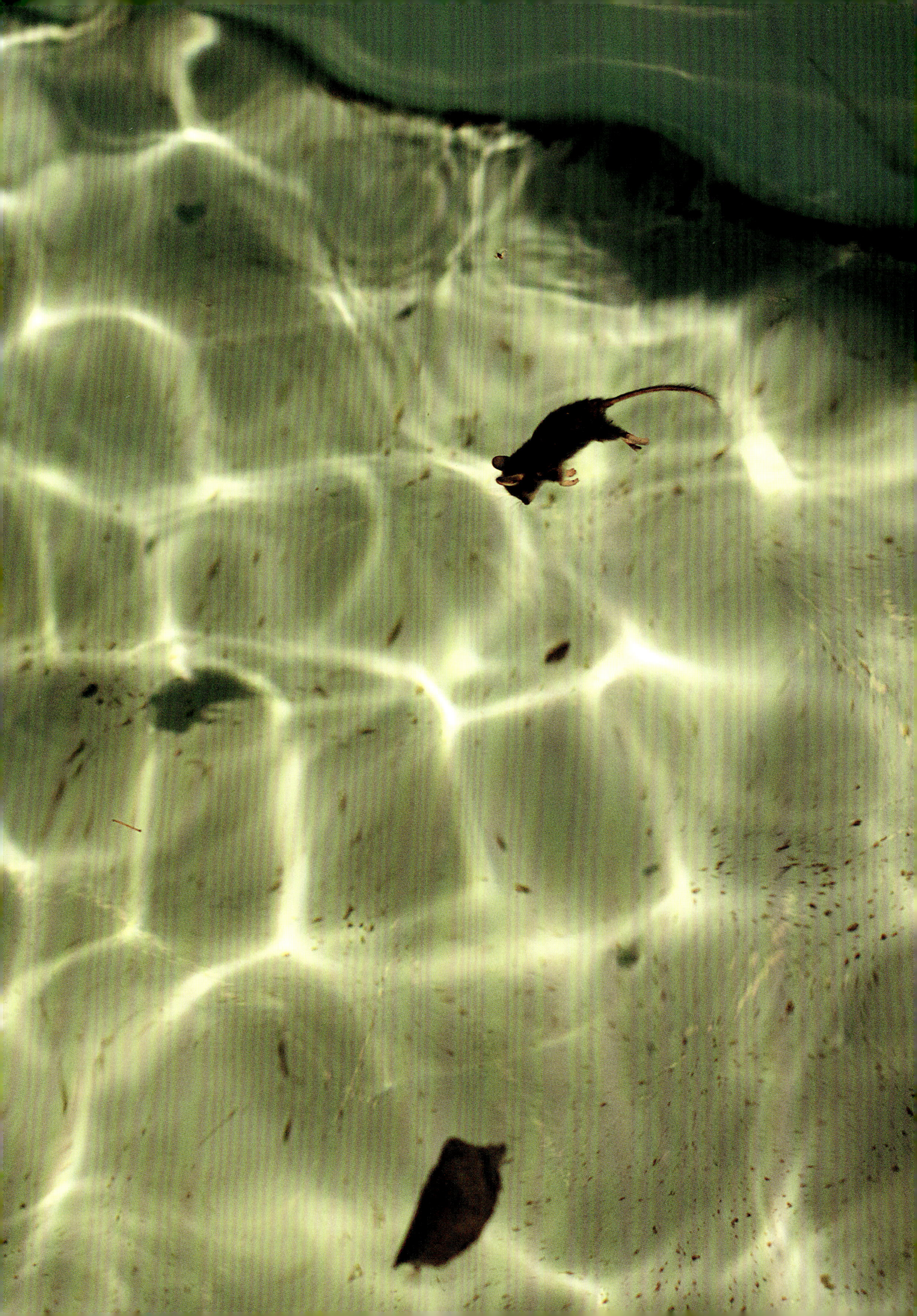

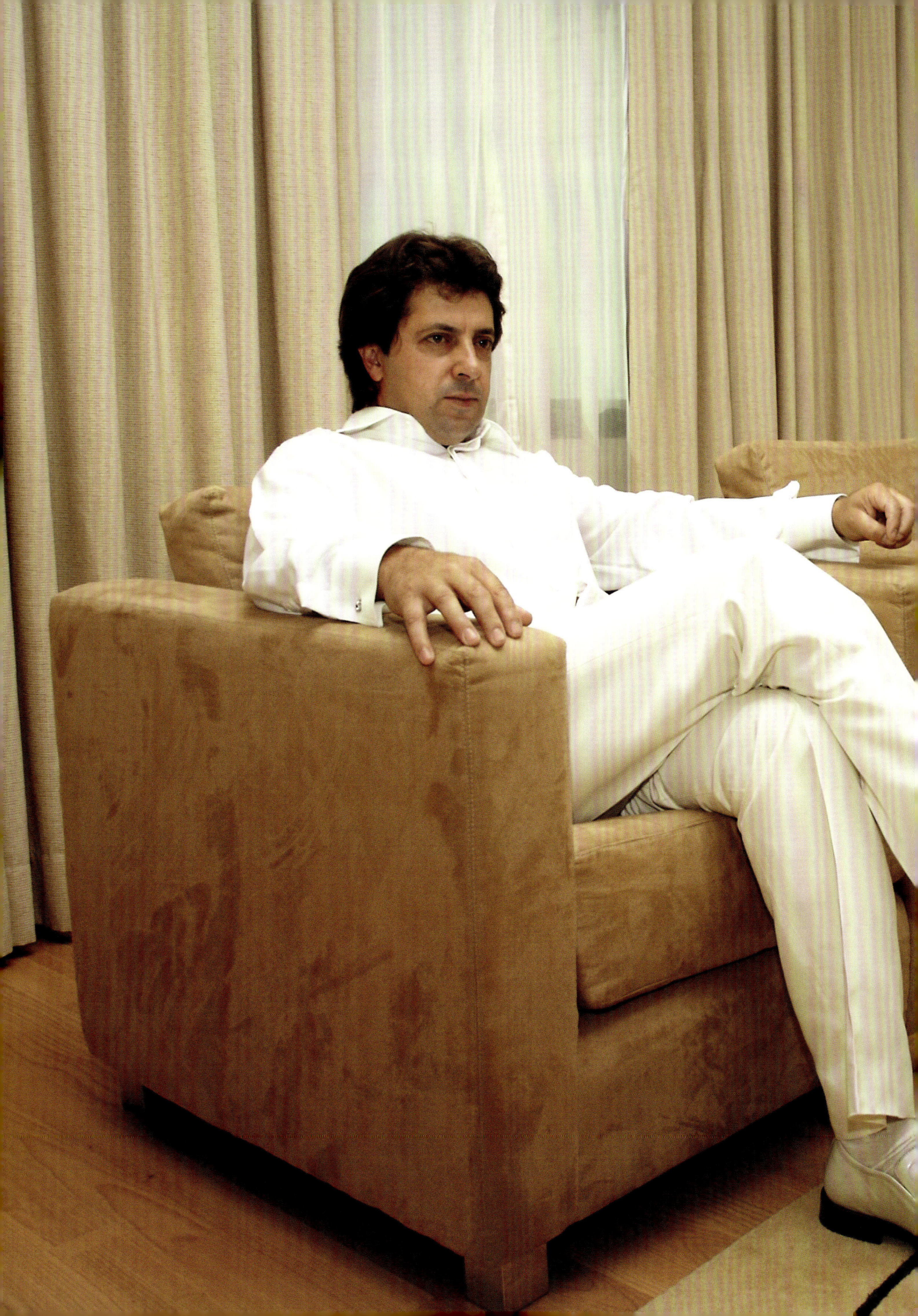

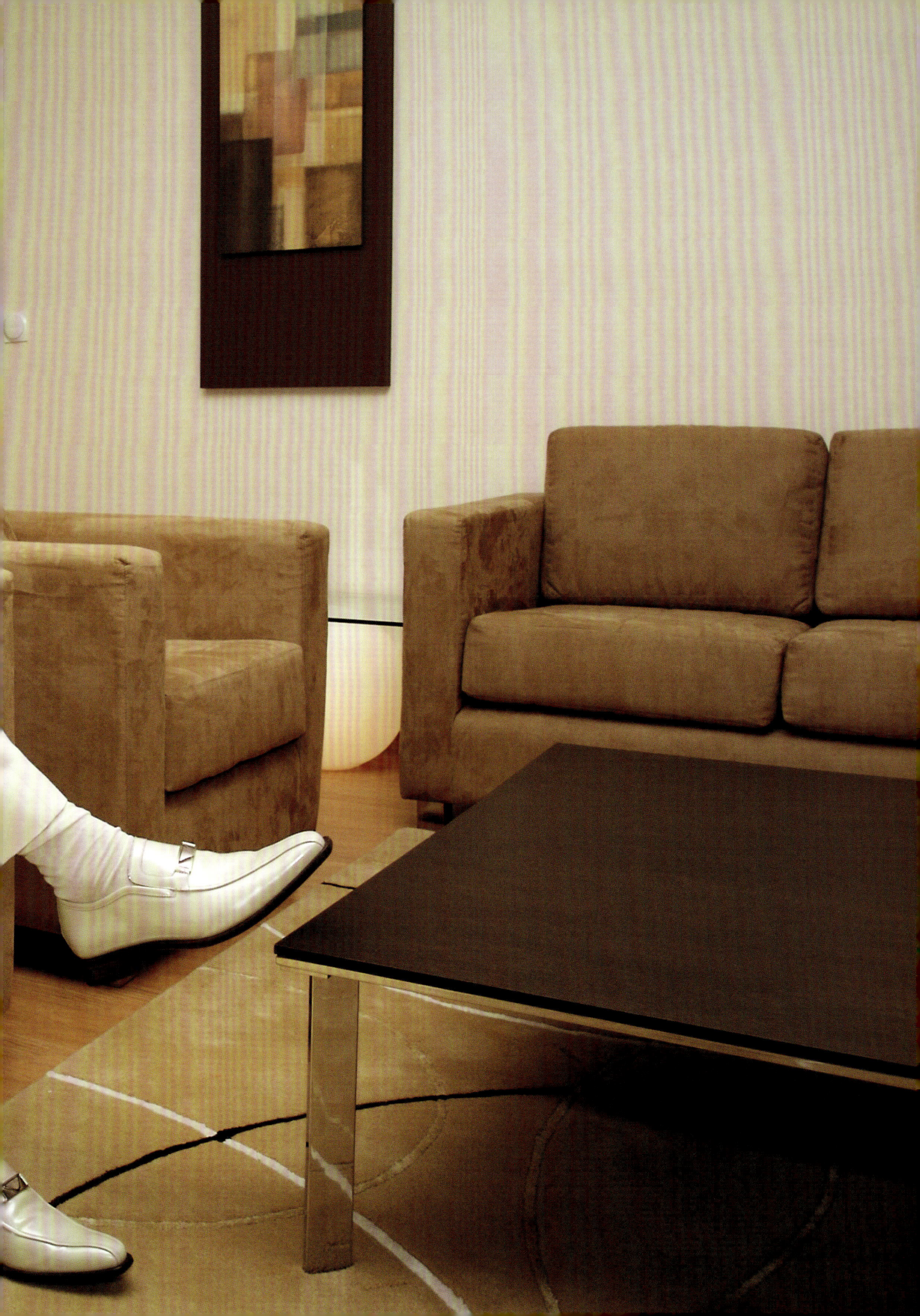

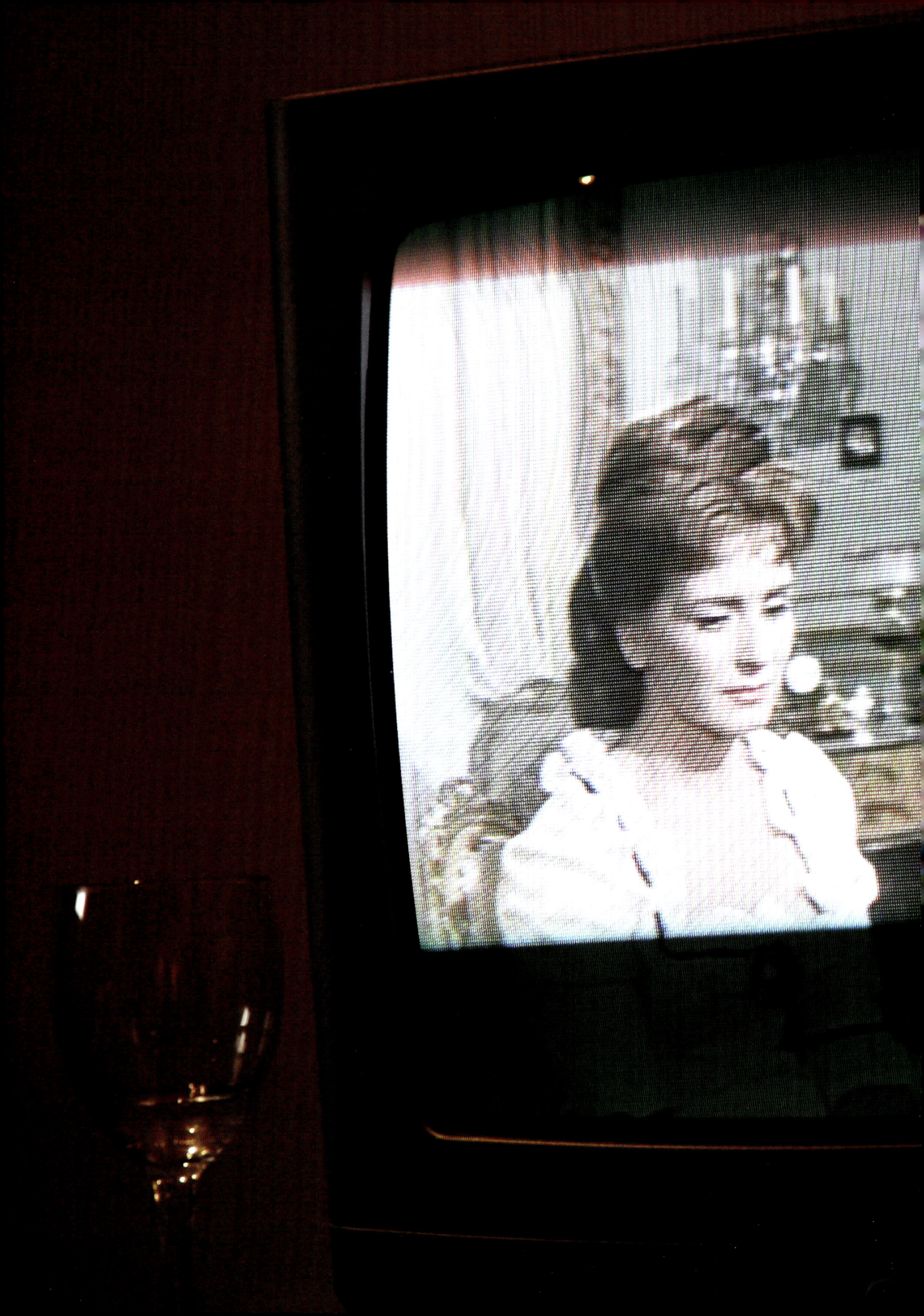

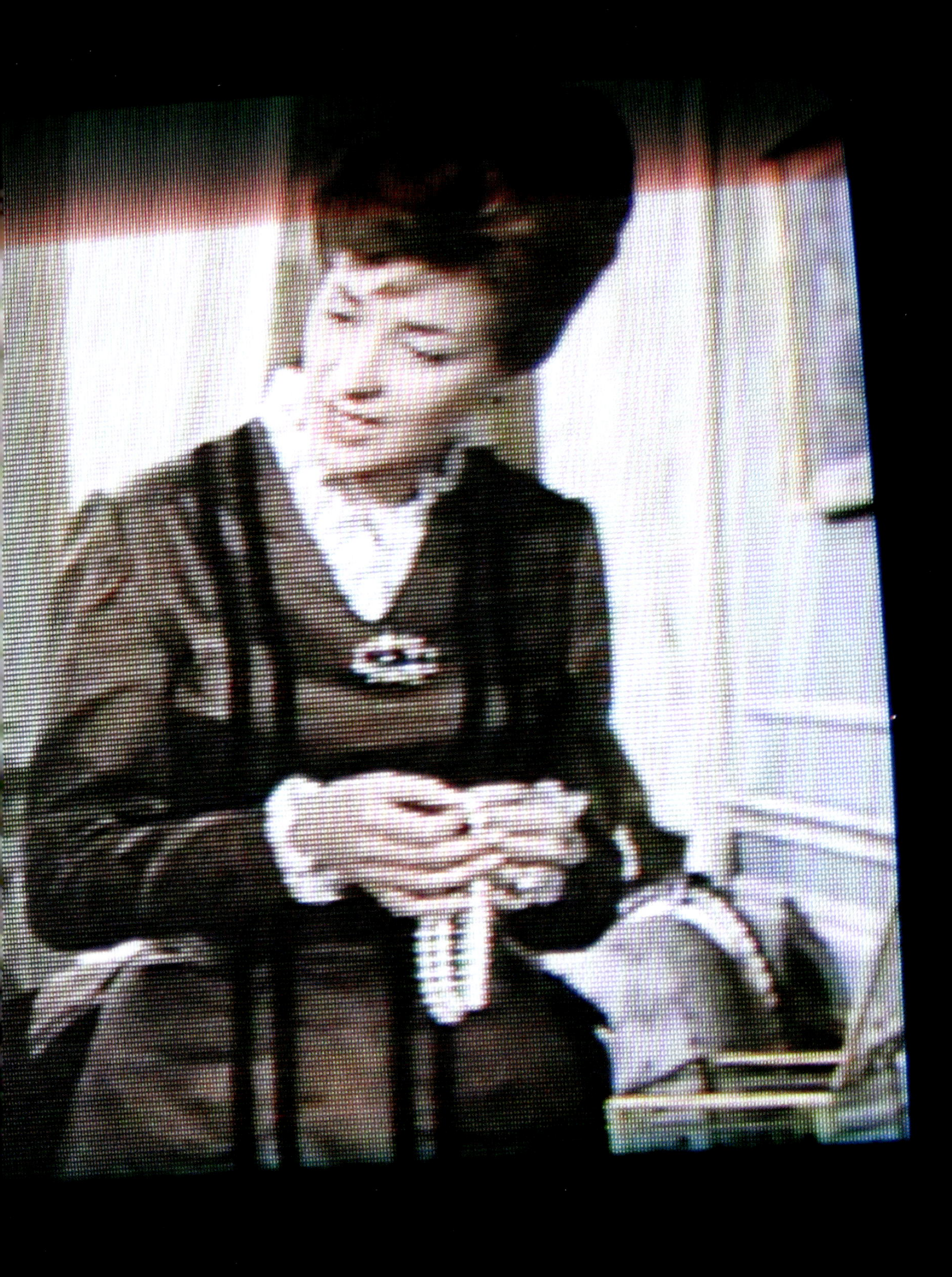

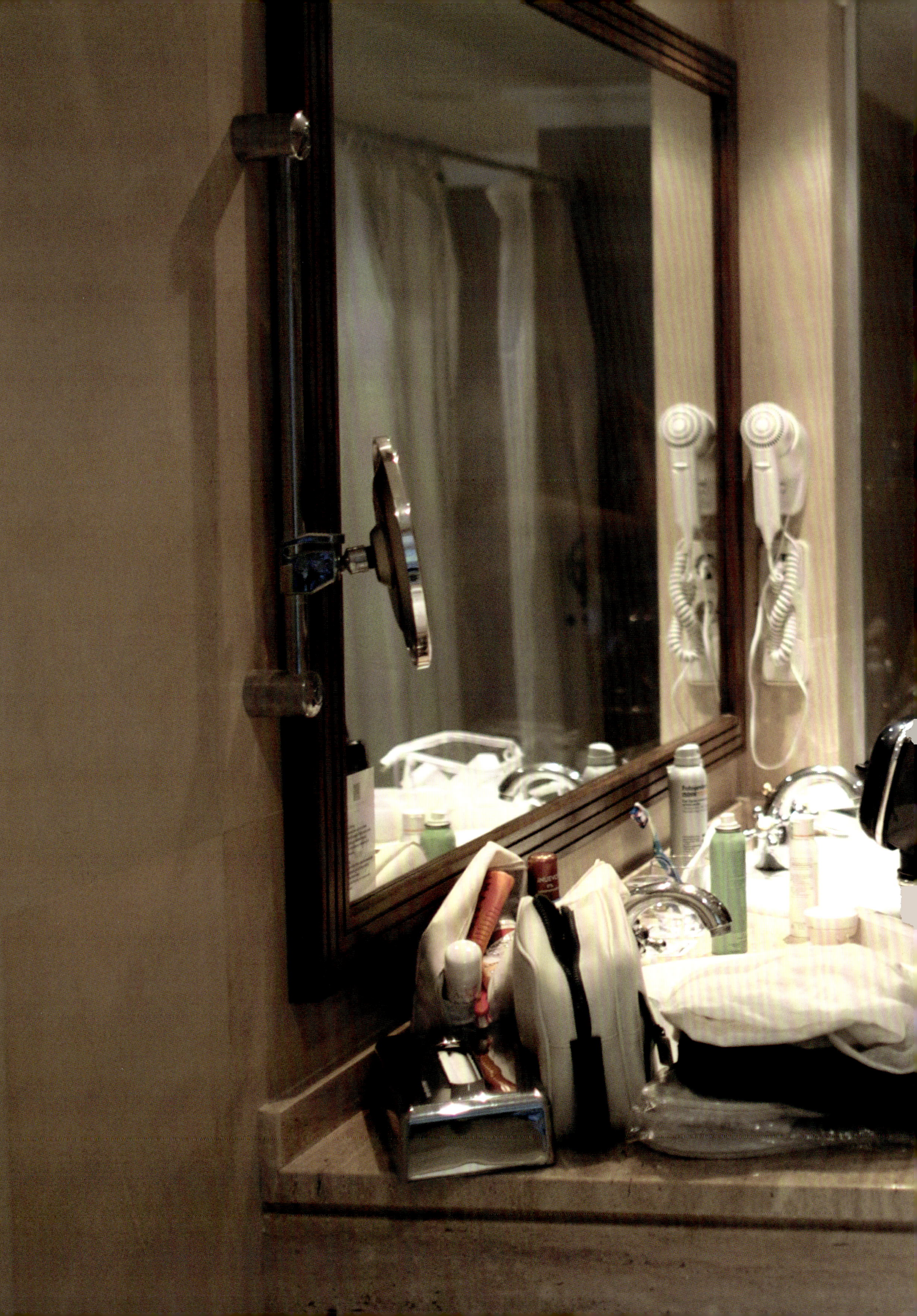

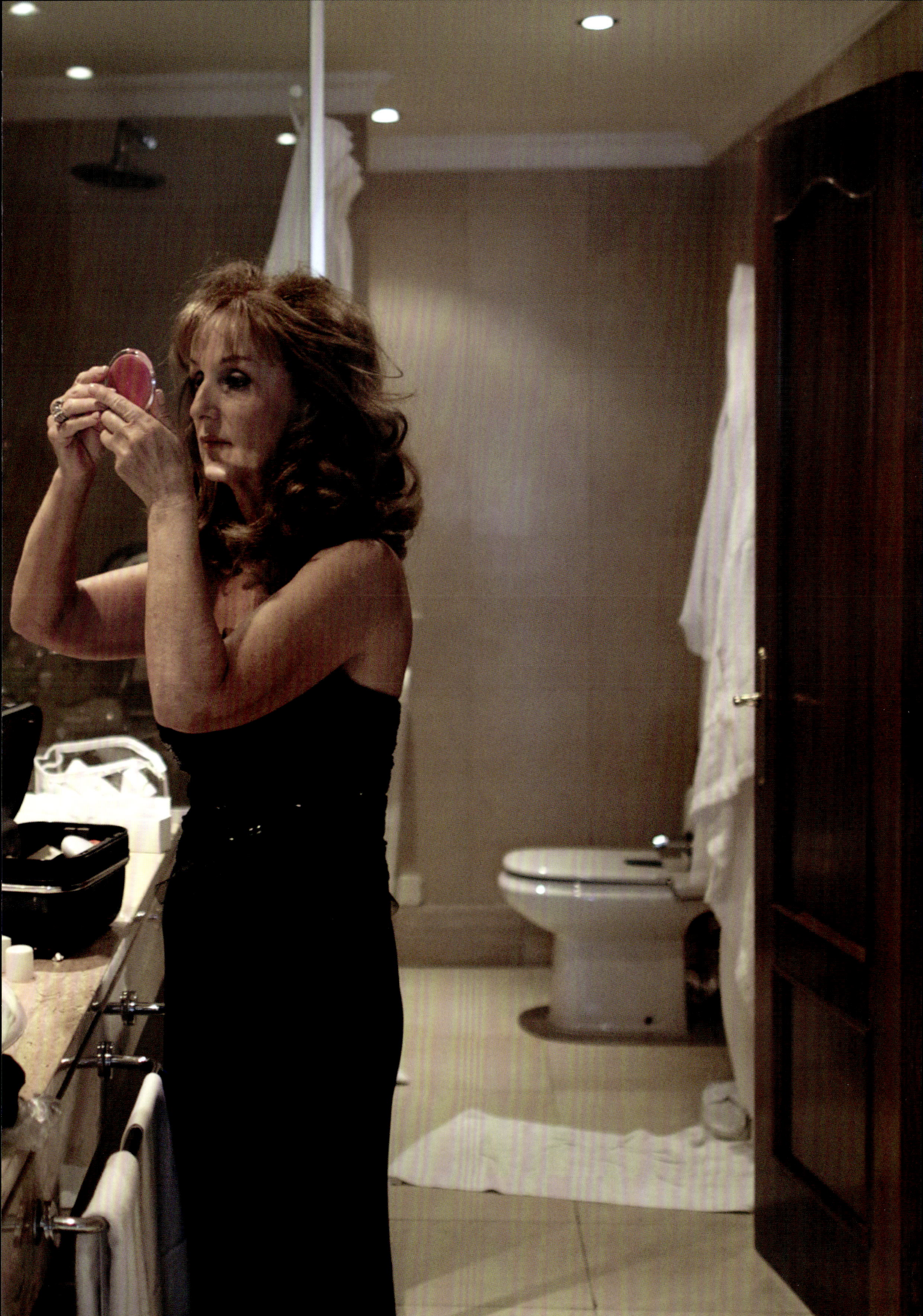

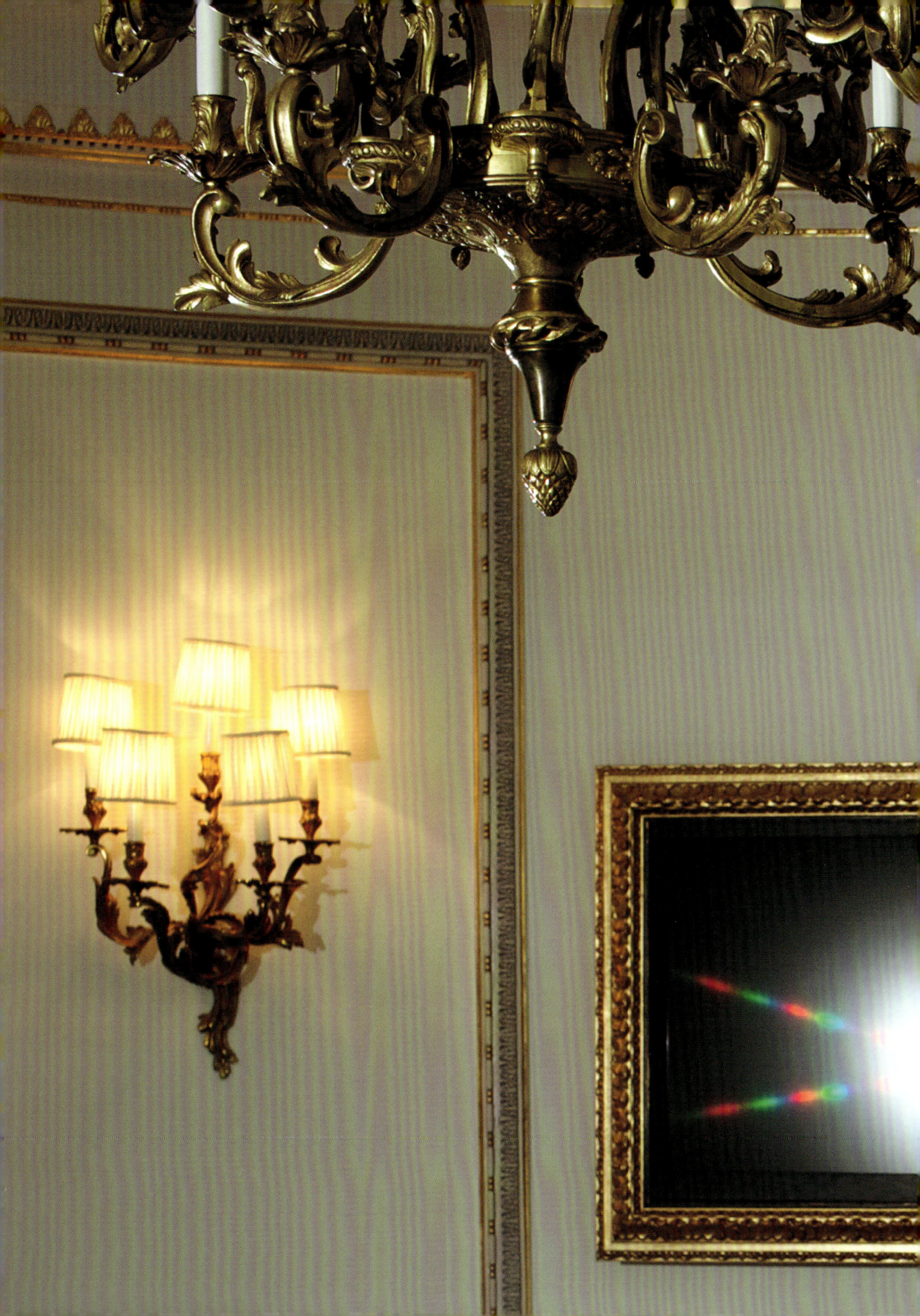

LG

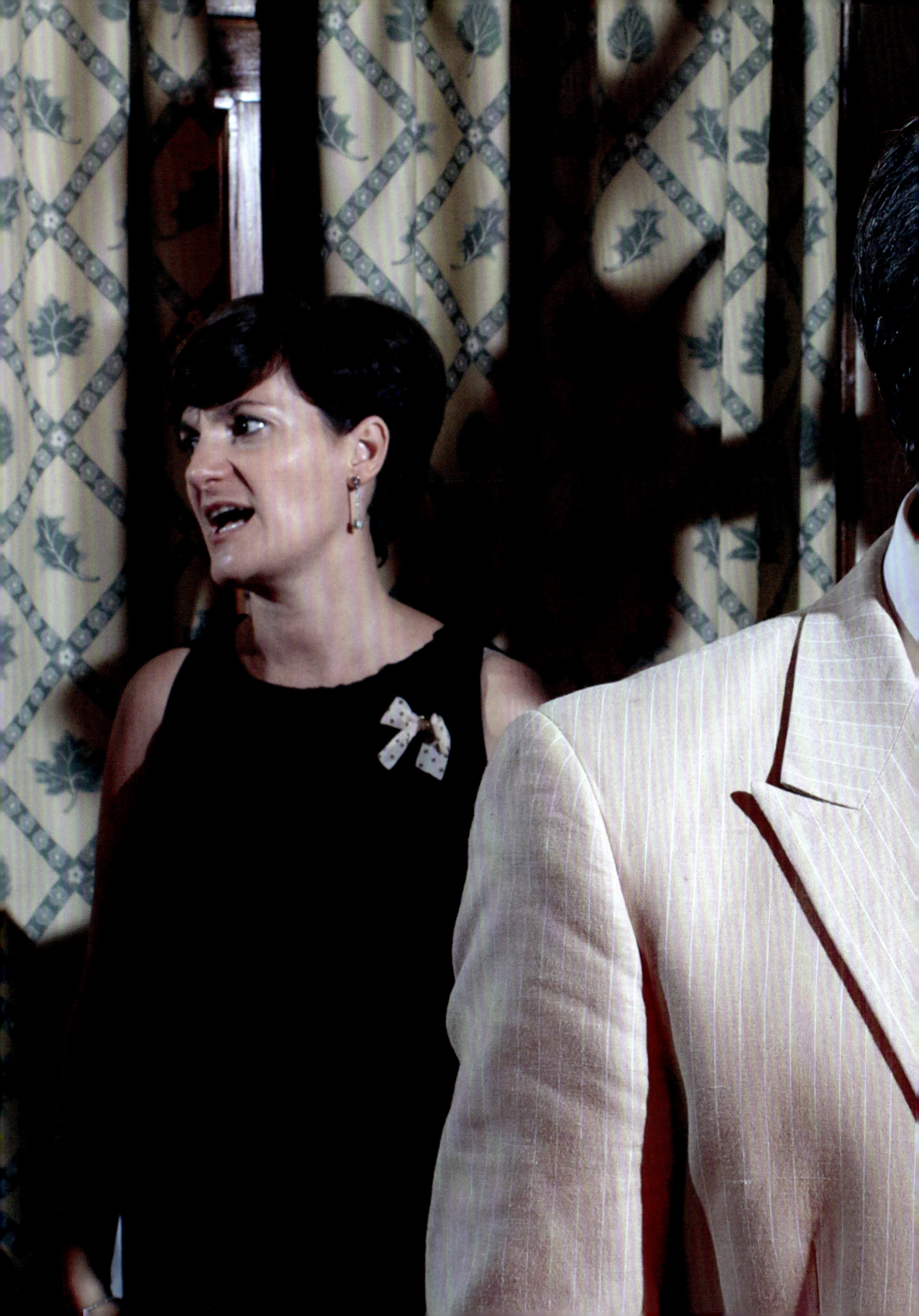

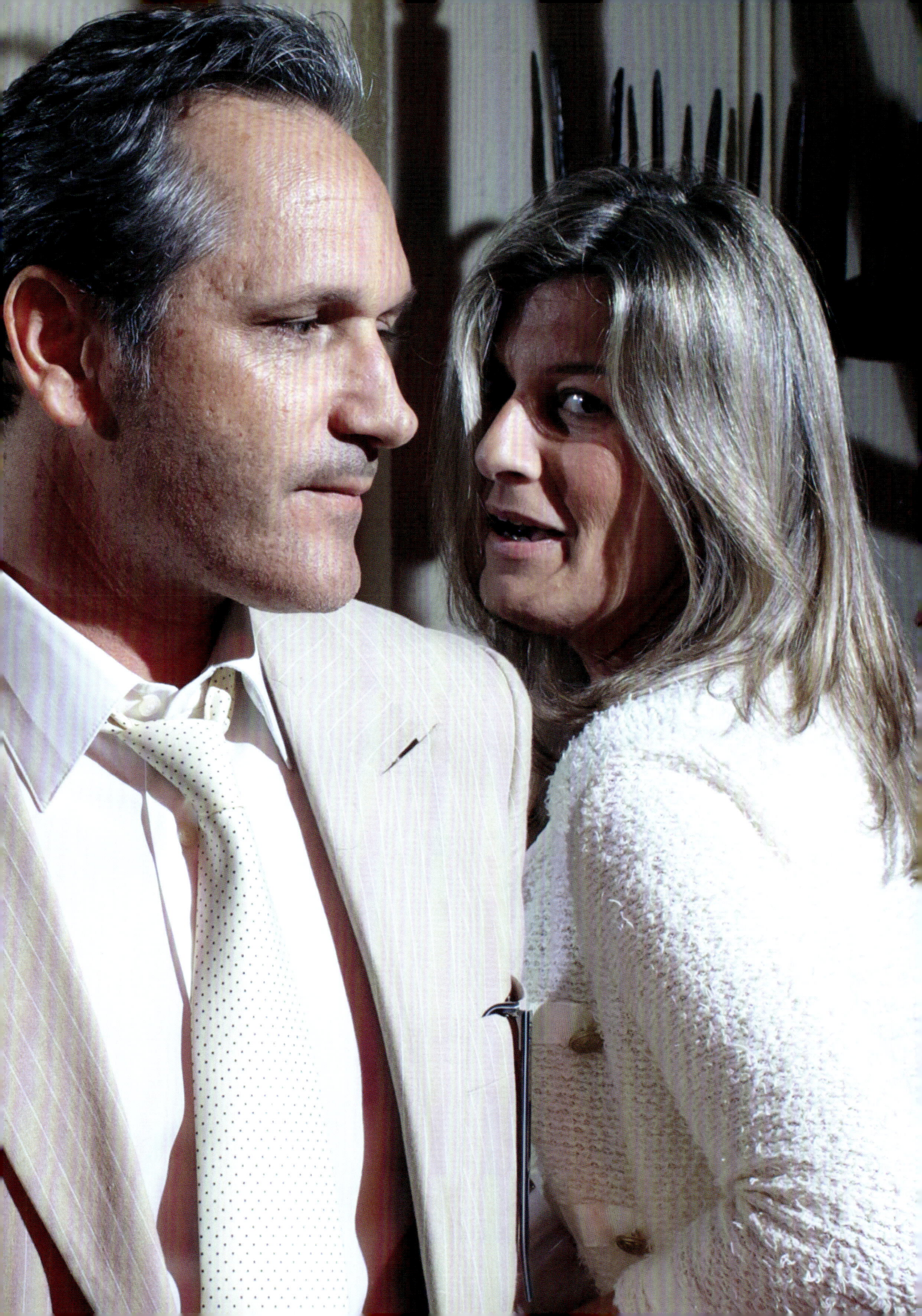

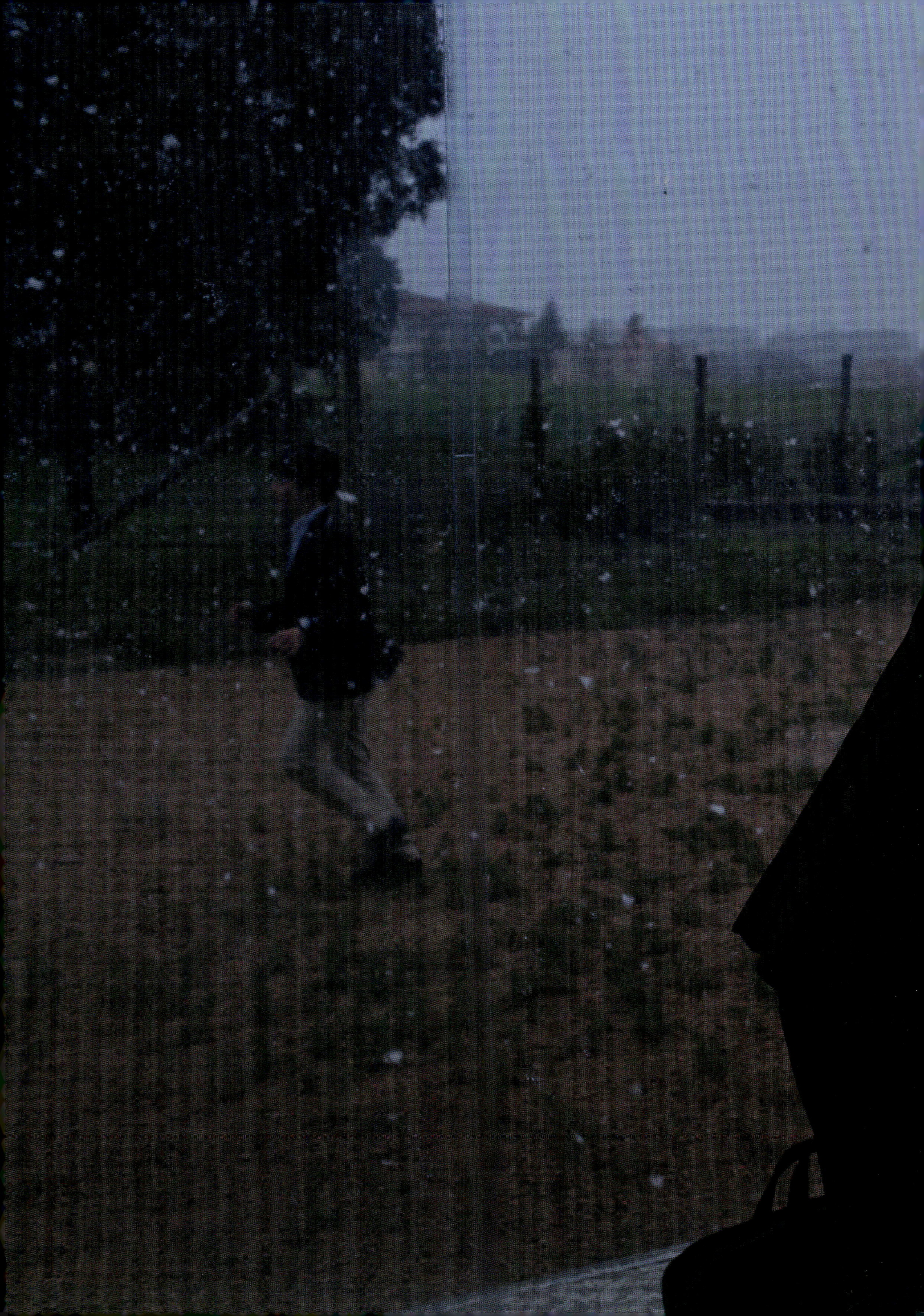

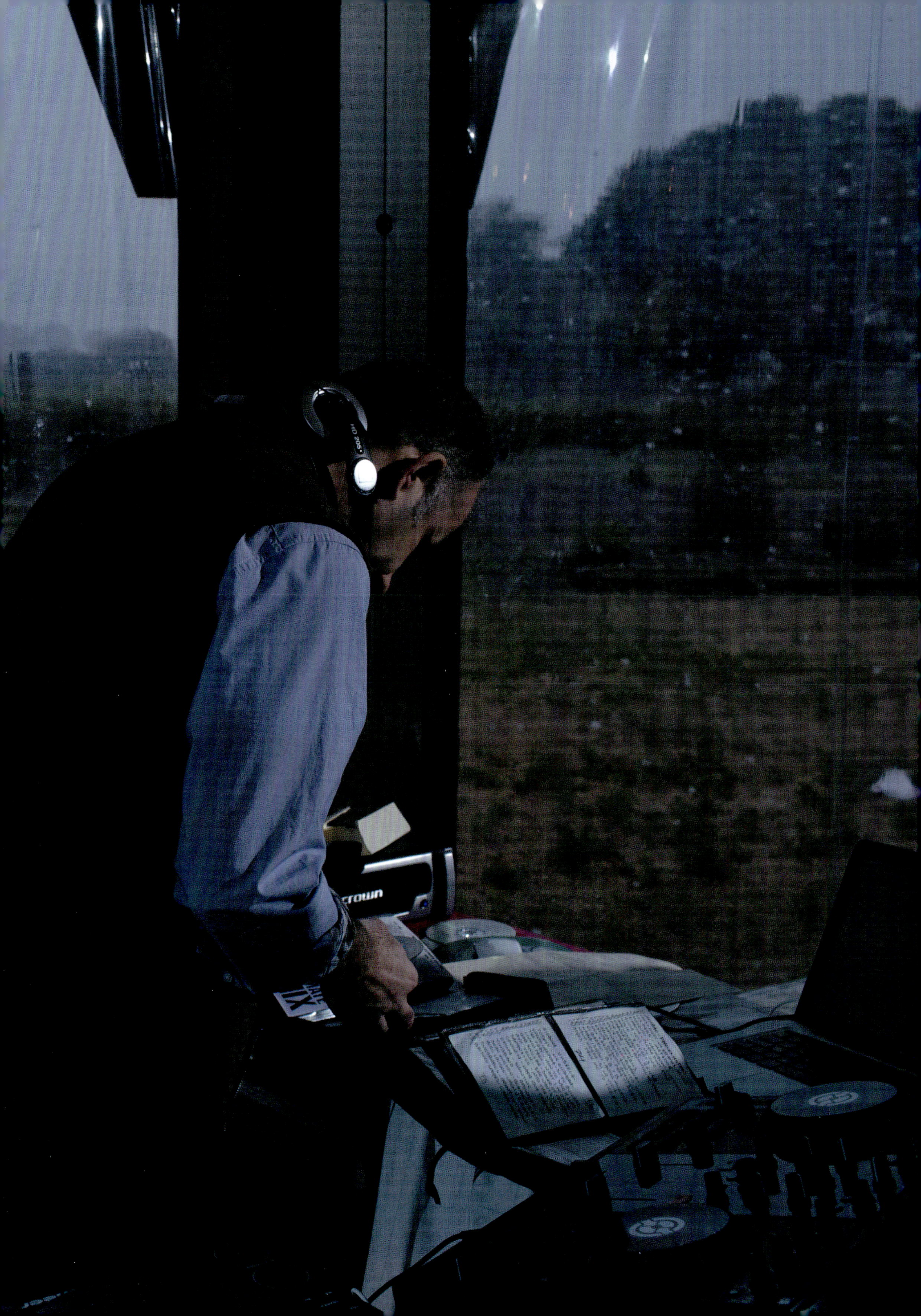
HD 205
crown

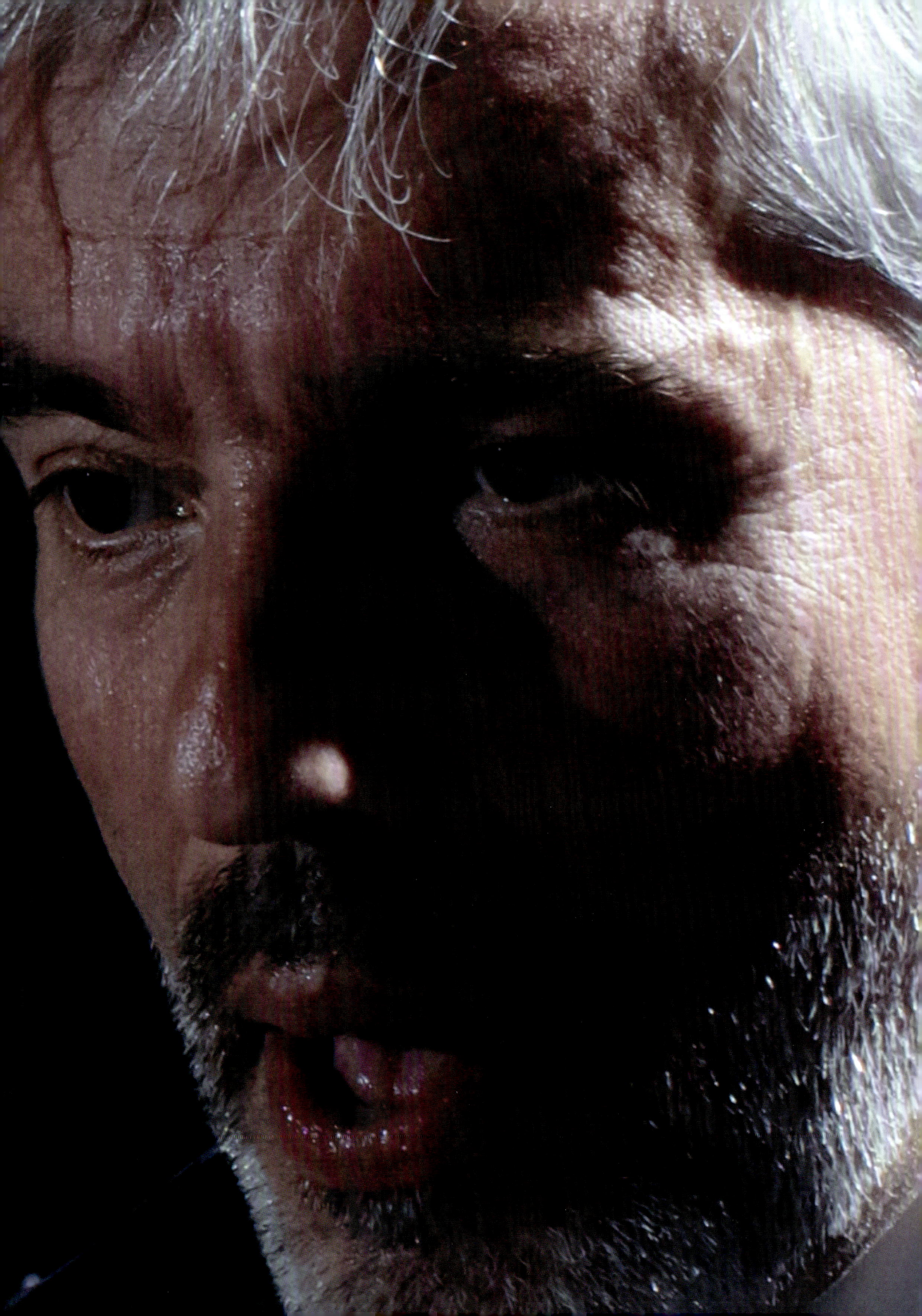

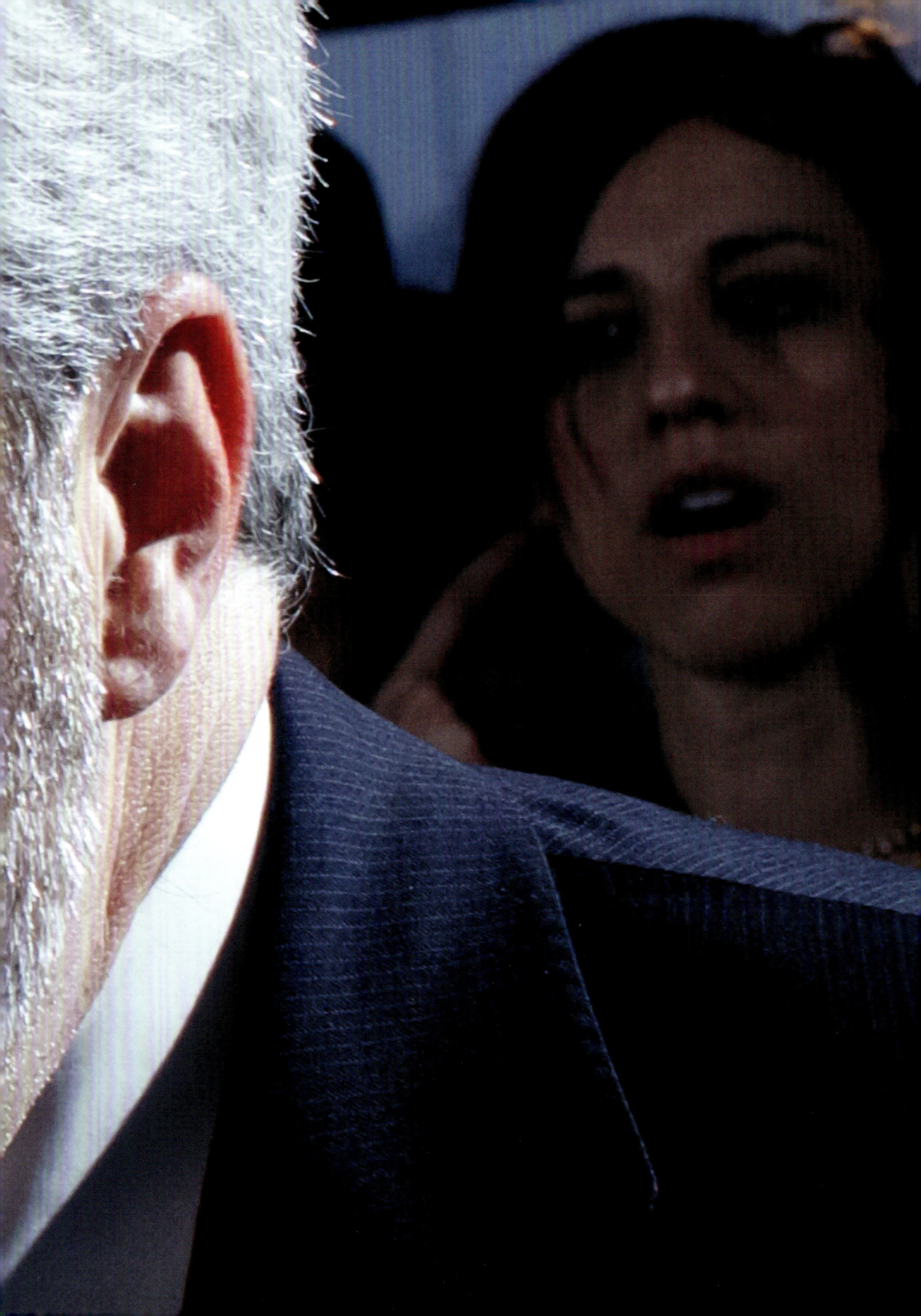

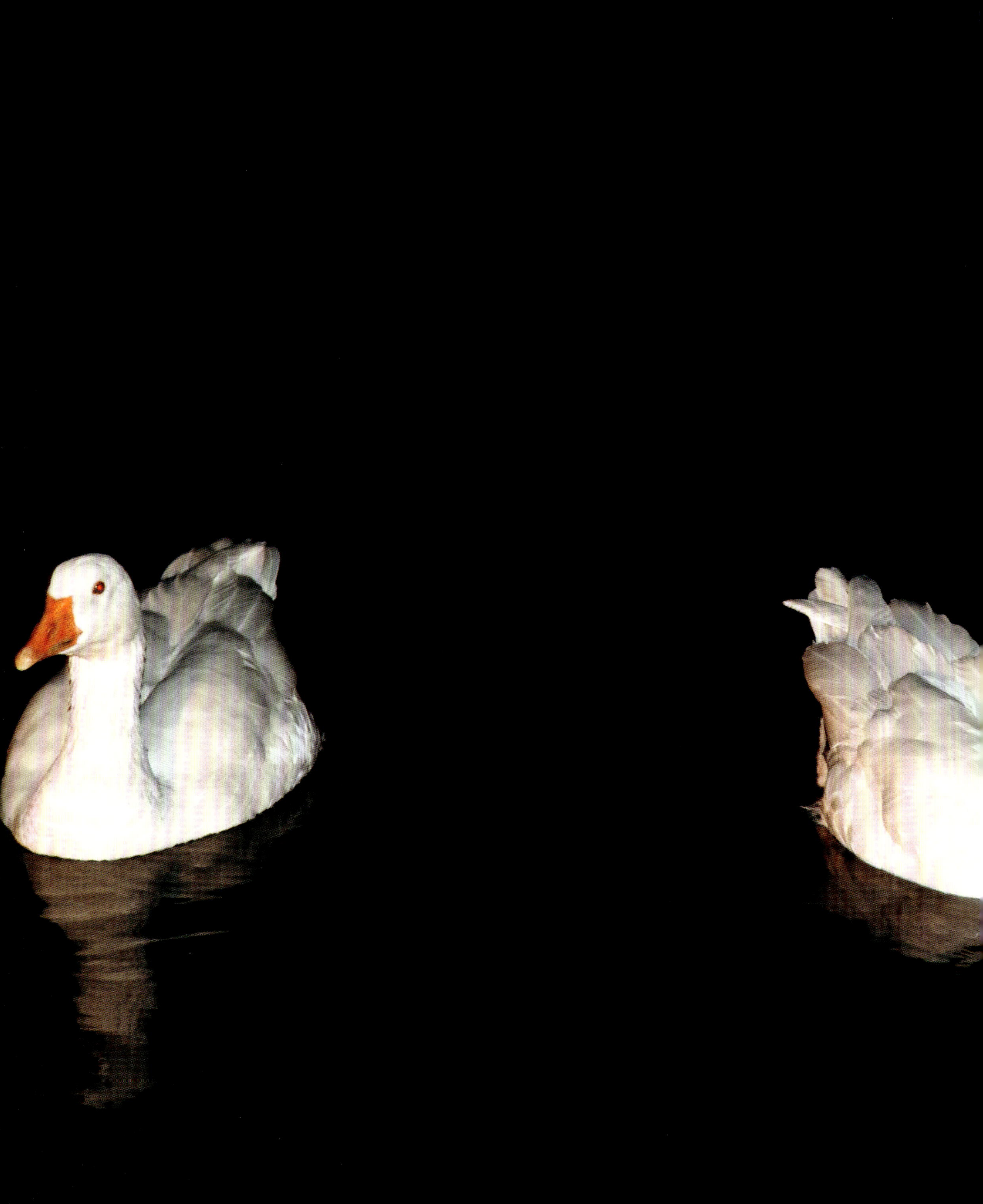

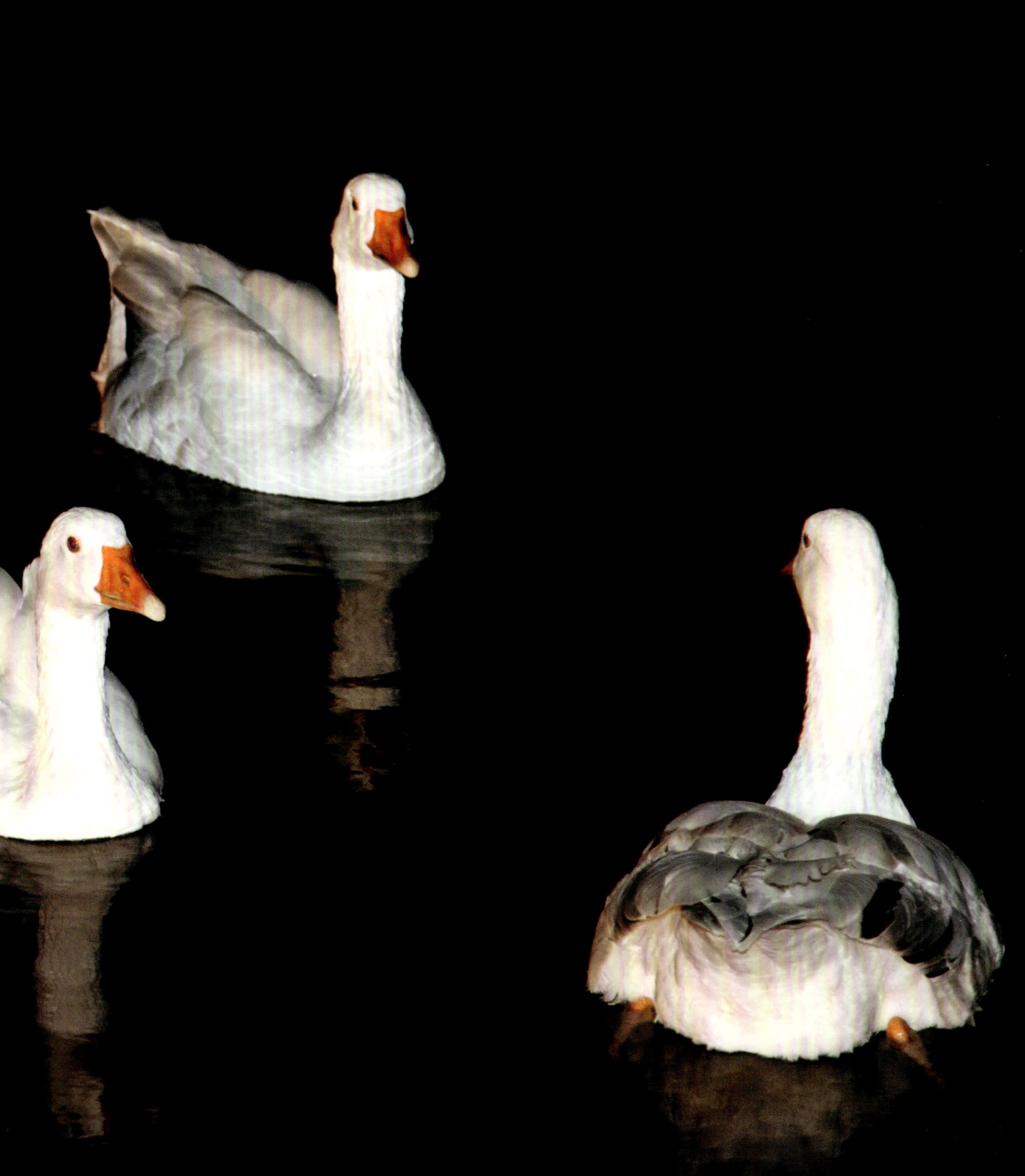

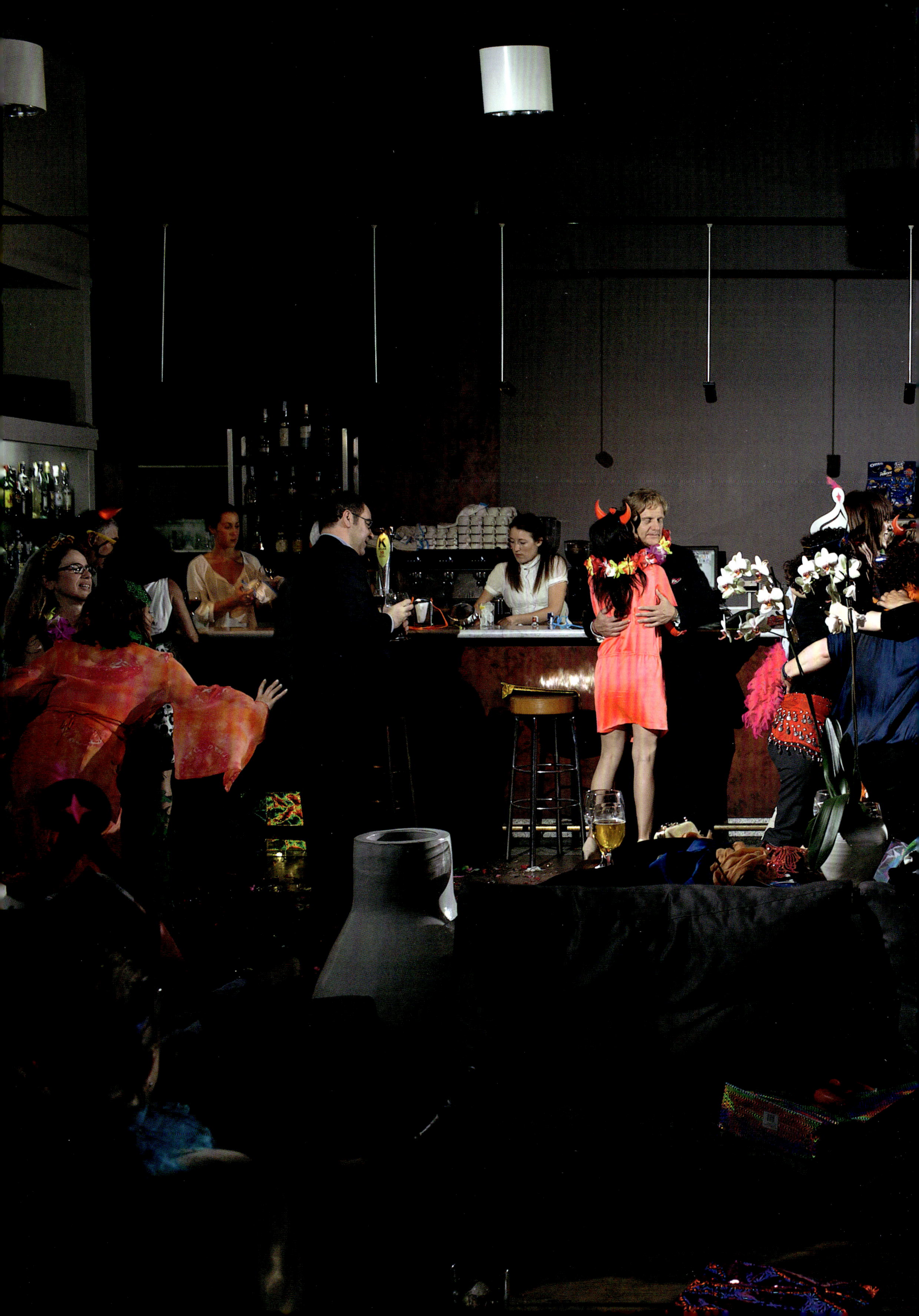

Mónica, this book is for you.
And it's because of you.

I want to express my gratitude for supporting my work to:
Eduardo Momeñe, Antonio Xoubanova, Nigel Bennet, Ricardo Cases, David Campany, Maria Jose Garcia Piaggio, Christopher Morris, José María Diaz-Maroto, Marcelo Augelli, Tatiana Martínez, Alberto Cabrera.

I would also like to thank everyone who made this book possible: Fotobookfestival Kassel, Dieter Neubert, Martin Parr and all the jury members of the Kassel Dummy Award 2017, Matthias Koddenberg and the Verlag Kettler team, Blank Paper, Gráficas Palermo, EFTI.

And to my family and friends: thanks for your love and encouragement.

This book has been awarded First Prize of the Kassel Dummy Award 2017.

Photographs and Concept Hugo Alcol

Editorial coordination Matthias Koddenberg

Typesetting Kristin Trüb

Production Druckerei Kettler, Bönen, Germany

Published by Verlag Kettler, Dortmund, Germany
www.verlag-kettler.com

ISBN 978-3-86206-674-2

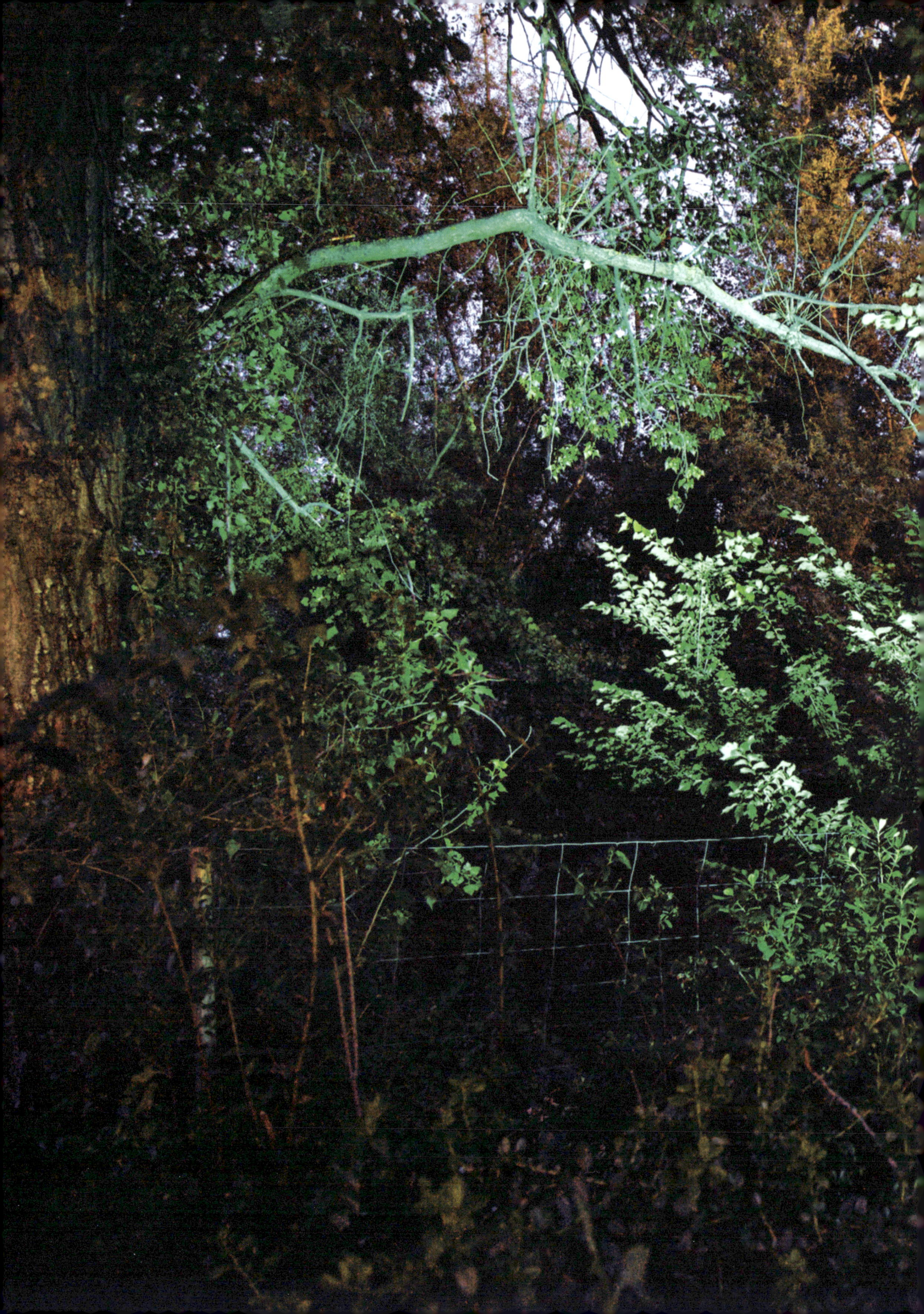